Keighley in th
Second World

C000181901

A shop-window display during War Weapons Week pushes a 'Bombers and Bombs for Victory' slogan. 'A Cash Bomb Will Fall As Each £100,000 Is Reached' declares the notice in the middle. 'Put Your Hand Down And Help To Drop The Whole Stick. Come On Keighley!' £600,000 has already dropped. *(Keighley News/Keighley Reference Library)*

KEIGHLEY IN THE SECOND WORLD WAR

IAN DEWHIRST

SUTTON PUBLISHING

Sutton Publishing Limited
Phoenix Mill · Thrupp · Stroud
Gloucestershire · GL5 2BU

First published 2005

British Library Cataloguing in Publication Data
A catalogue record for this book is available from
the British Library.

ISBN 0-7509-4165-0

Typeset in 10.5/13.5 Plantin.
Typesetting and origination by
Sutton Publishing Limited.
Printed and bound in England by
J.H. Haynes & Co. Ltd, Sparkford.

The Earl of Harewood, Lord Lieutenant of the County, taking the salute at the parade which opened Keighley's Salute the Soldier Week in 1944. The guard of honour in the foreground was provided by the Home Guard. *(Mr David Petyt)*

Contents

A wartime child – the author in 1943, sporting his toy National Fire Service tin hat. The belt was a relic from an uncle's First World War service with the Royal Naval Division. *(Author's collection)*

Introduction

On the eve of the Second World War Keighley was a not untypical West Riding industrial Municipal Borough, standing on the North Beck and the River Worth, adjacent to the River Aire and the Leeds and Liverpool Canal, and served by both the London, Midland and Scottish and the London and North-Eastern Railways. Developing its textiles, engineering and foundries from the Industrial Revolution onwards, by the twentieth century its manufactures included worsted, machinery and machine tools, gas and oil engines and wringing machines.

The Borough population at the 1931 Census had been 40,441, but a boundary extension in 1938, which brought in Oakworth, Haworth and Oxenhope Urban Districts, together with the East and West Morton portions of a former Keighley Rural District, boosted this to an estimated 58,000. At a stroke, too, the Borough acreage multiplied sixfold, from 3,902 to 23,611, though much of this was empty moorland sharing a westward boundary with Lancashire. There was no census in 1941, but the 56,000 ration books distributed by the Keighley Food Control Committee late in 1939 offer a clue as to the early shifting wartime population.

In so far as it was never actually bombed, Keighley itself did not have an especially dramatic or tragic war, although local aircraft crashes brought its reality much nearer than most townspeople were told at the time. Nevertheless, the town and district had to face all the changing circumstances and related problems experienced by every community at war. This book accordingly is an impression of life on the Home Front, and emphatically is not intended as a history of the Second World War itself.

Naturally the weekly *Keighley News* has proved invaluable. But during a period of restrictions, censorship and the need to bolster public morale, no newspaper can hope to present a full picture, so I have also used many original contemporary sources – Town Council and local societies' minutes, school logbooks, annual reports, diaries, some of them confidential at the time – that over the last forty years or more individuals and organisations have either lent to me or added to the Local Collection at Keighley Reference Library. I have also, though to a much smaller extent, drawn on some later reminiscences.

Wartime photography poses another problem. The case of three respectable members of the Keighley and District Photographic Association, who in 1942 were brought to court and had their films confiscated for innocently taking snapshots of a Warship Week procession, highlights both the zeal of the local constabulary and the dangers of pointing a camera in an unauthorised direction. Newspapers, when they published photographs at all, tended to confine themselves largely to cheerful worthy causes and fund-raising events.

A regular contributor to the *Keighley News* in the inter-war years was George A. Shore, who combined photography with a carpet and linoleum warehouse in Keighley Market. A member of the British Press Photographers' Association, he specialised in weddings and social functions. When wartime restrictions reduced his newspaper outlets, he continued to photograph groups – munitions workers, special constables, Home Guards – then sold prints to his subjects. He was obviously successful in this, as testified by the number and extent of his surviving work. The majority of the photographs in this book are probably by George A. Shore. Others are by William Speight, an engineer-turned-photographer who reached a similar arrangement with the local press and public. It has been doubly satisfying to find several illustrating social events that were originally reported without pictures.

The *Keighley News* must be thanked, not only for recording the local war as far as was allowed, but also for publishing for the past twelve years my weekly 'Down Memory Lane' feature, which has encouraged many readers to supply photographs and information. I thank editors Malcolm Hoddy of the *Keighley News* and Winston Halstead of the *Yorkshire Ridings* and *Lancashire Magazine*, in which some of my material first appeared; also the very many individuals who over the past four or five decades have lent or given me a variety of sources; and perhaps most of all the Keighley Reference Library archives, among which so much of my life, both at work and in retirement, has been spent.

This is the first time that a book of this nature about Keighley has been attempted, and I have been deeply conscious of ploughing a pioneer furrow, as regards both research and presentation, through a complex subject. To the best of my knowledge the facts are correct according to my sources, but any interpretations I put upon them are my own.

Ian Dewhirst
Keighley
October 2004

Chapter One

'A War to Stagger Humanity'

Keighley shares with Barrow-in-Furness, Skipton, Bradford, Leeds, Thorne and Cromer the doubtful distinction of a premonition of the Second World War as early as 22 May 1936. That evening the German zeppelin, the *Hindenburg*, appeared unexpectedly over the town, having altered the course of her regular flight from the United States to Frankfurt.

At 804ft long the biggest airship ever built, the *Hindenburg* was seldom as low or as close as she seemed, yet Keighley eyewitnesses could clearly read her

The *Hindenburg*, snapped over Westfield Crescent, Riddlesden, in 1936. *(Miss Doris Holgate)*

name and number, LZ-129, and distinguish her Olympic Games symbol (the 1936 Olympics were held in Berlin) and the swastikas on her tail. Those with cameras attempted snapshots, which generally fail to capture the full spectacle of the moment.

Poignantly, while over Keighley the *Hindenburg* dropped carnations and a crucifix to be placed on the graves, at nearby Morton Cemetery, of German prisoners of war who had died in the 1919 influenza epidemic. They fell within yards of the traditional centre of town, 'the spot where the old Cross stood, immediately adjoining the north-east corner of the Devonshire Arms Inn'. Clearly, somebody in Germany had done some homework.

Local opinion was immediately divided – was the *Hindenburg* simply 'a sort of friendly link between the two nations', or was she taking 'aerial pictures for use in the event of war'? She flew over again that June, as well as over the Midlands and along the south coast. She was debated in Parliament, and the question of her unofficial flights was taken up with the German government. A *Yorkshire Observer* defence writer thought 'it would be stupid if on each trip they don't have ten or a dozen of their Air Force pilots on board. It is a wonderful opportunity for German pilots to look at our country and to take note of the "landfall".'

Suspicion was part of the atmosphere by 1936. Even the *Keighley News* carried such headlines as 'The War Peril', '"No" to Fascists' and 'The Next War: Plans for Protection in Air Raids'. That August the Keighley Corporation, in common with every other local authority in the county, received a letter from the West Riding County Council seeking to coordinate 'precautionary measures' and requesting information on planned decontamination centres, mobile first-aid and rescue groups, casualty clearing stations, fire brigades and ambulance services.

That same year Keighley's Town Clerk, Medical Officer of Health, Fire Brigade Chief Officer and chairman of the Watch Committee attended a Leeds conference of local authorities on the subject of air-raid precautions, although it was to be the beginning of 1938 before the Corporation's preliminary scheme was submitted to the County Council. Meanwhile an official was sent to a Civilian Anti-Gas School at Easingwold to qualify as an instructor and set up a training centre for Council staff and volunteers.

In 1937 the Morton Banks Sanatorium became home for Basque refugee children from the Spanish Civil War; and in 1938, when Yorkshire's German residents held their annual memorial service at the prisoner-of-war graves in Morton Cemetery, they controversially gave the Nazi salute. They also laid a wreath on the adjoining British war memorial.

That spring Keighley's first air-raid wardens joined special constables and regular policemen for the first time under one roof for a dinner and an address

by the Chief Constable and Air Raid Precautions (ARP) Officer of the West
Riding, followed by singers and a comedian. The event was deemed 'a splendid
opportunity of getting the three forces together so that they could get to know
one another and talk things over'. Another thousand volunteers were called for,
although a month later only seventy had come forward.

Early that August the works of paper-tube manufacturers J. Stell and Sons
Ltd were assessed as to their 'capacity for the production of armament stores'.
At this stage, working double shift in the event of emergency, their weekly
quota (though 'required for record purposes only') was to include 2,000
'Containers Cartridge B.L. 6″ Gun Mark I. M.L.' and 2,000 'Containers
Charge Aircraft Catapult Mark I'.

Also in August an ARP Officer was appointed for the Keighley, Bingley,
Shipley and Denholme Joint Area. He was Stanley Noel Jenkinson, who had
previously been Northern Area ARP Organiser for Leicestershire and held a
commission in the Royal Scots Territorials.

The Keighley district was deemed to require 114 ARP posts, each manned
by six wardens. Despite the deteriorating European situation, only some two-
thirds of the requisite 684 wardens had enrolled by late September 1938,
though informal lunch-break talks in mills and workshops had speeded the flow
of recruits. Fifteen men had volunteered as auxiliary firemen.

Meanwhile people sunning themselves in Devonshire Park 'received a mild
shock' at the sight of a hundred men and women in gas masks. These were
volunteers from industry and local government who had qualified as
decontamination instructors, having completed courses on 'asphyxiants or lung
irritants, nasal irritants or arsenical smokes, lachrymators or tear gases,
vesicants or blister gases, paralysant gases, gases liable to be encountered under
war conditions and fumes which may be encountered in fire-fighting'.
Thankfully, human nature soon translated such jargon into a more accessible
form:

> Things have come to a pretty fine pass
> When we have to go round a-smelling for gas,
> But if war comes, and smell we must,
> All ARP Wardens will know, I trust,
> That a nasty smell of musty hay
> Does the presence of Phosgene gas betray,
> Whilst bleaching powder's irritant smell
> Tells the presence of Chlorene gas quite well.

Towards the end of September 1938 the Czech crisis injected a dramatic
sense of urgency into warlike preparations. The local view of foreign affairs is

nowhere more succinctly expressed than in the handwritten records of Knowle Park Congregational Church, whose meticulous Minute Secretary headed a page 'Of National Importance':

The last week in September was a momentous one, as this country along with Czechoslovakia, France and Russia were on the very brink of war with Germany, whose Dictator 'Hitler' had threatened immediate invasion of Czechoslovakia, in the same manner as his troops invaded Austria a few weeks ago.

Some Reservists and Territorials were called up. Keighley's 6th Battalion the Duke of Wellington's Regiment, though not mobilised, went on alert. There were some local recruits for the new Women's Auxiliary Territorial Service, and the total number of ARP volunteers leapt up to 827, including 646 wardens; first-aid workers rose from 12 to 50, auxiliary firemen from 15 to 38.

Air-raid trenches were dug in public parks (at Silsden they utilised an old tunnel for farming stock crossing under Bolton Road), and respirators were hastily distributed. Basement windows at Keighley Public Library were protected with sandbags. On a spiritual level, local churches held services of intercession.

'Our Prime Minister, Mr Neville Chamberlain, had the courage and wisdom to seek a personal interview with Hitler,' wrote the Knowle Park Minute Secretary, outlining the events leading to 'an agreement which ended in a promise to settle the dispute by arbitration, Czechs having at the suggestion of Britain and France agreed to the terms laid down to surrender the Sudeten German territory to the Reich . . . '.

Opinions were divided. The Keighley Communist Party met in the Town Hall Square and passed a resolution that 'called on Labour to resist the Chamberlain Government's betrayal of democratic Czechoslovakia by any means in its power'. A Keighley Peace Council organised a public discussion in the Britannia Hall, which attracted such a crowd that another was simultaneously held outside for the overflow. A young Denis Healey 'doubted whether anything had been done at Berchtesgaden for Czech injustices'. Keighley Rotary Club wrote to its Prague counterpart expressing its members' 'profound feelings of sorrow and sympathy' over 'the great misfortune and national calamity which befell the Republic of Czechoslovakia by the notorious Munich Pact'.

Yet 'day by day' a *Keighley News* editorial voiced the feelings of probably the majority of ordinary folk, who 'clung desperately to the hope that war would be staved off', and by October 1938 felt able to offer this reassurance:

With the historic Four-Power Conference at Munich on Thursday the peace hopes of practically the whole world were realised, and with the signing of the pact early yesterday morning millions must have thanked God that a war that had threatened to stagger humanity and claim millions of lives had been averted.

The Knowle Park Minute Secretary echoed the hope 'that the Prime Minister has saved the world from one of the worst catastrophes ever known'.

In an immediate mood of relief the Temple Street Methodists held a thanksgiving service, rendering the 'Te Deum' and singing 'There's a Light upon the Mountains'. One grateful citizen donated £1,000 as a 'thank-offering for the blessing of peace' to endow a bed in the Keighley and District Victoria Hospital; another, £50 towards furnishing new children's wards. The hospital cannily published a list of further requirements, and more gifts flowed in. Thousands visited a Peace Exhibition in the Municipal Hall, and schools celebrated a Peace Week.

Notes of caution were struck, however. The trenches in the parks – which had promptly flooded during a three-day storm – were to be completed then 'widened, lined, and roofed with concrete' before being covered with earth and levelled, awaiting possible use. A thinly attended ARP meeting was told that although 'the emergency appears to have passed there is to be no slackening in the efforts in Keighley's Air Raids Committee'. A volunteer medical corps was formed. A gas-proof room was created in the basement of an empty house in the centre of town, open for public inspection and emulation. Cracks in the walls, ceiling and woodwork had been 'stopped up by means of sodden newspaper or putty pasted over with gummed paper'; even mouse-holes were plugged. The Keighley Conservative Women's Association heard an address on 'The Crisis – Its Causes and Effects'. The speaker, while concluding that 'the German people wanted war least of anyone', warned of 'the necessity for this country's rearmament'. A local appeal on behalf of the Lord Mayor of London's fund for Czechoslovakian refugees closed at £339.

If, for many, life seemed largely to resume its normal tenor, much was quietly happening. True, wardens at neighbouring Bingley enjoyed a jolly New Year dance, with the band topically playing behind a mock trench, but meanwhile the joint Keighley, Bingley, Shipley and Denholme ARP was taking delivery of 275,000 sandbags, which were stored in the erstwhile Union workhouse together with other equipment and 20,000 civilian respirators. Keighley was classed as a reception area in the event of evacuation, to which end a census of householders was compiled. The government issued a National Service Guide listing the many and varied defence organisations.

This comprehensive group of members of the Grove Mills ARP Volunteer Services, photographed in September 1940, was enlarged, framed and hung in the office at Robert Clough (Keighley) Ltd. *(Mr E. Smith)*

There was a county-wide testing of air-raid sirens, showing Keighley's to be unsatisfactory, leaving a number of 'dead spots' unwarned. A new 'Gent' siren was accordingly installed over the Coney Lane electricity works and operated from the fire station. For good measure, the warning was carefully explained as 'warbling signals, varying in pitch, and of two minutes' duration', and the 'All Clear' as 'a continuous high-pitched signal of two minutes'.

Employees of the Keighley Corporation Waterworks Department were taught how to deal with bomb-damaged mains. The Water Engineer, J. Noel Wood, designed a galvanised iron water-supply tank for emergency use; it could be handily fitted to a waterworks lorry and held 300 gallons which could be drawn from twelve cocks.

By April 1939 an impressive ARP parade was able to muster a thousand local volunteers, comprising 'uniformed auxiliary firemen hauling trailer pumps, first-aid parties, motor drivers, special constabulary, air-raid wardens and workers in supplementary services, together with fire engines and ambulances, several rescue squads on lorries, an emergency water carrier, and a van carrying a portable chlorination plant'.

One conflict, at least, came to a controversial close – the Spanish Civil War. That May the Revd J. Nicholson Balmer, minister at Devonshire Street Congregational Church and Chairman of a Yorkshire Joint Committee for

Spanish Relief, escorted thirty-three of Keighley's Basque refugee children back home as far as the Spanish frontier where, invited to dinner with three Fascist officers, he 'thought his own thoughts when they toasted General Franco'. The children could sing 'On Ilkla Moor Baht 'At' and 'Lambeth Walk'. Sixty-six of their compatriots remained at the Morton Banks camp because of difficulties in tracing their parents.

On 3 June the Military Training Act required males aged 20 to 21 to register for National Service, an exercise which in Keighley yielded 183 potential militiamen and 3 conscientious objectors; Haworth produced 70 militiamen, Silsden 20. The young men who registered were described as 'of a smart type'.

By midsummer 1939 the Keighley Section of the Women's Voluntary Services for Civil Defence had opened an office, giving advice and encouragement to those considering the many available options in ARP: evacuation, billeting, transport, hospital and food supplies, auxiliary nursing. . . . The response was 'gratifying'. Factories were being advised to organise their own emergency cover. Boy Scouts holding pathfinder and cyclist badges were asked to join their newly formed messenger service.

Yet despite increasing numbers, some volunteers were failing to train conscientiously and 'the view was expressed', at an August review of the past three months' progress, 'that in time of international crisis enthusiasm for the work was high, but as the crisis receded interest was apt to fall away'.

Less than a fortnight later, Germany invaded Poland and, on Sunday 3 September, Britain entered the Second World War.

Changing its tune from the previous year, the Knowle Park Congregational minute-book heaved a metaphorical sigh of relief: 'The country is solid in its determination to make an end of this state of terrorism and dictatorship, and to stand for freedom and democracy.'

Chapter Two

'Civil Defence – Urgent!'

War at its outset was an unknown quantity. Keighley cinemas closed during the first week, and the Technical College postponed enrolment for its evening classes. The Keighley and District Victoria Hospital sent some patients home and restricted admissions. Silsden Show was cancelled. But once the Board of Education had recognised the need for cultural activities in wartime, the Workers' Educational Association started a slightly delayed autumn session, offering solid courses on psychology, physiology and social philosophy. In a more practical vein, classes the following spring were on nutrition in wartime.

When the cinemas reopened (Keighley had six, and there were two at Haworth and one at Silsden), a slide was projected onto the screens: 'Civil Defence – Urgent! You can help by joining the "life-givers" brigade, and registering as a member of the blood transfusion service . . . You May Save a Life. It is Harmless. Do It Now.'

Street lighting went out. Most of the factories at Silsden dispensed with a breakfast break so as to make fuller use of daylight. Street corners and causeway edges were painted white, and pedestrians wore white armbands or waist-belts in the blackout. Indeed, Keighley had already suffered its first blackout casualty on the night of Saturday 2 September, when an elderly widow was fatally injured in the dark by a slow-moving double-decker bus with regulation-dimmed lights.

Keighley Town Councillors promptly re-timetabled their committee meetings for daytime hours 'as a temporary expedient until the volume of the ordinary work of the Council becomes more normal'. Their Museum Curator reported how he had spent £7 on measures for 'the protection of exhibits in the event of an air-raid', while the Chief Librarian gained approval for revising the hours of opening and closing his branch libraries and reading-room, owing to 'present lighting restrictions'.

As the wintry nights closed in and the blackout became an increasingly potent inconvenience, the Borough Electrical Engineer was instructed to install low-intensity lighting in the town centre, giving priority to lamps 'in the vicinity of the homes of the permanent firemen and near to the fire station'. He also designed an experimental illuminated kerb edge which was 'hollow and contained a light that showed through two slits at the front'. Two were tried at a pedestrian crossing on Station Bridge. 'Keep to the Left' slogans were painted on the pavements of main streets, 'with a view to minimising mishaps'.

Gas masks became obligatory, but initially many people were reluctant to carry them openly, preferring to hide them in shopping-bags or wrap them up into brown-paper parcels. The cardboard boxes in which they had been issued were inappropriate for a wet climate, 'old camera and field-glass cases being recommended instead'.

'On receipt of an Air-raid Warning,' proclaimed the Corporation Gas Department, 'gas consumers are advised to turn off the gas at the meter'. Householders with Anderson shelters were told to erect them at once; those without were advised to acquire 'a considerable degree of protection by digging a trench in the garden with 18 inches of overhead earth cover' – twenty-six families at Barley Cote, Riddlesden, combined to construct what was 'probably one of the most efficient' air-raid shelters in the district, 70yd long and 7ft deep.

Even ordinary houses were thought to offer a good deal of protection 'unless a big bomb falls very close indeed'. When the gable-end of two back-to-back houses in Bradford Street and Bingley Street noisily collapsed early one Sunday morning, the neighbours feared it was a bomb and followed instructions by staying indoors rather than rushing out to investigate! 'People', ran one dubious reassurance, 'should not be upset by pictures of what happened to the poorly-built houses in Spain'.

Pessimistically foreseeing 'the possibility of having to deal with damaged sewers as a result of enemy action', the Borough Engineer laid in a quantity of spare pipes of various sizes. The Borough Architect was subsequently authorised to spend £1,513 on 'slate and other roofing materials for the repair of houses which may be damaged', and another £70 on twenty 9yd ladders. Water tanks were stored at the Open-Air School.

Moore's chemist's, 'near the Picture House', ran a timely but thought-provoking advertisement: 'Immediately after the "All Clear" signal goes, at any time of the day or night, our shop will be open for the sale of first-aid requisites.' Another amenity of questionable value in terms of morale was 'a mortuary for Keighley civilians who might unfortunately be killed during the period of hostilities'.

It is sobering to reflect that, had the Luftwaffe bombed Keighley, they would have known where their targets lay. Two maps of the area were brought back from Germany after the war. Comprising a north and south sheet, each headed 'Town Plan of Keighley with Military Geographical Entries', the maps are basically enlargements of our own 6in Ordnance Survey, with the German grid system superimposed. Heights 'over low water at Liverpool or Newlyn' are given in 'English feet'. Information in German around the margins includes a table for converting feet into metres.

Issued, for service use only, by a Department for War Maps of the German Army General Staff, they purport to show the 'situation in 1940', though the note 'Edition No. 2' suggests there had been an earlier version. A separate heading meticulously states: 'Military geographical data according to documentary evidence available on 30 April, 1942.'

Closer study reveals that the Germans were not quite up to date, even if they were using our latest available Ordnance Survey. Sewage works alongside the River Worth are marked as belonging to Oakworth and Haworth Urban Districts, which had in fact merged with Keighley Borough in 1938. The Westgate area is shown as having been cleared, but Oakworth Road still turns right into Bridge Street instead of crossing the North Beck to High Street. This dates the basic map to the mid-1930s.

Otherwise, German thoroughness is impressive. Both plans are covered with symbols in red, purple and black to indicate points of special interest. Even the key to the symbols, printed down a margin, is exactly appropriate to each map. Brewery and tannery signs appear only on the southern sheet, which highlights Knowle Spring Brewery and Parkside Tannery; warehouses and gasworks only on the northern sheet, which includes Aireworth Shed and Thwaites.

Particular attention is drawn to industrial sites, individual premises being specified as engaged in textiles, engineering or iron-working. Naturally, the industrial parts of Keighley proper bristle with appropriate symbols, but the Germans have not omitted such peripheral targets as Oakworth, Lower Providence and Vale Mills. Even Woodlands Mill at Steeton and little Wood Mill, deep in Holme House Wood, have been noted. The Phoenix Foundry, out at Beechcliffe, warrants an ominously prominent highlight all of its own. In the case of Castle Mill on the North Beck, German intelligence had been faulty – shown as producing textiles, Castle Mill had turned instead to furniture manufacture years earlier.

Keighley's main reservoirs lay beyond the scope of both maps, but smaller sources of water supply are indicated at Black Hill, Highfield, West Lane, Calversyke Hill, Whinburn and Cross Roads. Even a small reservoir or 'earth container' in the middle of Alder Carr Wood has not been missed. Similarly, a comprehensive rash of quarries is shown at Bogthorn, Braithwaite, Parkwood, Hog Holes Brow, Hainworth and Hainworth Shaw, Steeton and Nanholes near the Guide Inn.

Keighley and Ingrow railway stations and goods-yards are prominent, as is the 'bus depot', by which is meant not the bus station but the bus garages off Suresnes Road.

Bridges are separately identified, according to whether they carry roads or railways. Here the Germans have marked in black not simply the obvious Stockbridge, Aireworth Road and Dalton Lane, but also such details as Lodge

Hill Bridge over the Leeds and Liverpool Canal near Alder Carr Wood, and the East Avenue and Cemetery footbridges over the railway. Little Damems station emerges prominently, boasting both a bridge carrying a road and a bridge carrying a railway, to say nothing of Damems Mill working on textiles beside it. Several bridges below Oakworth serve to draw unwelcome attention to the Worth Valley Railway, as the Cross Roads tunnel does to the Great Northern line.

As one ponders the implications of such memorabilia, a crumb of retrospective comfort is derived from the Germans having indicated the Keighley and District Victoria Hospital and the West Riding County Hospital boldly in red. Theoretically, in the event of an air raid they would have tried *not* to hit them!

Fortunately Keighley was not put to this test, but in 1939 public air-raid shelters intended primarily for those caught outside during raids were an obvious priority, although it was October before some at least really took shape. This was a subject on which a restricted local press could enlarge, for people needed to know where to make for in an emergency.

There were concrete trench shelters under the Town Hall Square (to accommodate 250), the brand-new High Street roundabout (200) and Victoria Park (550). Strengthened basements with emergency lighting and exits were strategically sited round the town, mostly beneath well-known business premises like the Keighley Industrial Co-operative Society Ltd in Hanover Street, ironmonger's J.W. Laycock Ltd in North Street and W.H. Burns's music shop in East Parade (though such refuges, the public were cautioned, 'will not withstand a direct hit'). Some houses in Sun Street, scheduled for demolition, were converted instead into surface shelters.

The Town Hall Square shelters roused 'considerable dismay' because they entailed the destruction of mature trees and shrubs. More in Devonshire Park were slow in completion, and a Town Council minute from May 1940 revealed that Keighley's shelter programme was still lagging: 'Resolved – That the County Council be asked either to complete or fill in the trenches in Lund Park in order to give this portion of the Park a more tidy and pleasant appearance.'

The Keighley Education Committee debated at length 'the best measures of safety for school children', inclining at first towards their being 'dispersed to their homes' in the event of a daytime raid. 'Can you imagine', expostulated one member, 'an air-raid warning being given and the confusion that would be caused by turning out onto the streets over 6,000 school children when fire engines, motor-ambulances, and motor-cars driven by special constables are busy plying the streets, and when air-raid wardens are carrying out their duties in ordering the public off the streets!'

Despite this shocking scenario, a mixture of school trench, basement and surface shelters was still under construction a year later, while provision for

Worth Valley pupils was still at the discussion stage – school windows, at least, were to be protected 'by the application of muslin'. Entrances to trenches in the Boys' Grammar School playground were at first insufficiently shielded, and the decision not to fix doors on elementary school shelters meant that teachers on playtime duty were tasked with trying to keep children out, for they would chug happily round the dark catacombs as 'ghost trains' in imitation of a popular funfair entertainment.

In the meantime Holycroft Council School sent parents a duplicated letter headed 'Air Raids, during School Hours', advising that children could be sent home, or to friends or relations, if living within five minutes of school. 'All other children will remain in the care of the teachers,' this missive sternly declared. 'Will you please note that on no account should parents come to the school in search of their children since this might upset safety arrangements and increase danger to all concerned. Please see that Gas Masks are always brought to school.'

The care provided by schools could initially be basic. Worth Valley churches were invited 'to loan seating accommodation for school basements, etc., where no other special provision has been made'. When the Holycroft Juniors tried an air-raid practice early in 1940, 140 pupils went home, while the rest 'went to their places in the cellars etc.'. The 142 children who stayed for Ingrow Council School's first practice were split between the local Congregational Mission, the Corn Mill, the caretaker's house and the school itself; 227 went home.

At Horkinstone Council School at Oxenhope the staffroom was adapted as a shelter and equipped with a lavatory, 'also a tin of disinfectant', and later a 'drinking-can'. At least – by 1941 – windows inside and out were covered with anti-splinter muslin and netting.

At Eastwood Council School, however, a sense of greater urgency prevailed, possibly because of its situation in a thickly residential district cheek by jowl with potentially targetable industrial sites. 'Children who live near school were sent home and told to return,' reveals the head teacher's businesslike logbook early in the war. 'Time checked to find out how long it took them to get home.' Before September 1939 was out the pupils had practised putting on gas masks every day for a week.

To begin with, the school's temporary air-raid shelters comprised the cellars of the local Co-operative Society stores, but on 13 October 1939 the Borough Architect, the Director of Education and the Chairman of the Education Committee 'came to school to discuss positions of Air Raid Shelters'. By the beginning of 1940 playtimes had to be curtailed 'because the playing space is small – trenches are being made in the playgrounds'. In May the pupils were able to make 'a tour of four air-raid shelters now available for Junior Scholars in school yard', and by June they were having practices every Wednesday between 9 and 9.30 a.m., when the children learned to 'run quickly and orderly to shelters'.

Public reassurance was of paramount concern. 'All the various defence services are in working order', the *Keighley News* had stressed at the outset, 'and every man and woman knows his or her allotted task'.

This boast was, however, not entirely true. At the outbreak of war in Keighley the Auxiliary Fire Service and the Special Constabulary were indeed up to strength, but more air-raid wardens were still needed, as were auxiliary nurses, Territorials and volunteers for the Women's Auxiliary Territorial Service and the Police War Reserve.

An element of tardiness was to be repeated in 1941 when registration for Civil Defence duties was made compulsory for male civilians aged between 18 and 59. Keighley and Haworth Employment Exchanges duly processed some 10,500 men, of whom 80 per cent tried to claim exemption! It is only fair to add that those who served acquitted themselves satisfactorily a year later during a simulated invasion designed to test the efficiency of air-raid wardens, first-aid parties and demolition squads working in conjunction with the military and the Home Guard.

Now, however, recruiting accelerated – to the extent that so many ex-servicemen aged 45 to 55 applied to join a National Defence Company that the British Legion Club ran out of entry forms.

Activities in the autumn of 1939 were many and various. Week by week in the local press Boy Scouts were given enterprising ideas as to how they could contribute to the war effort: 'The elderly people in your neighbourhood might be very glad if you whitened their steps and door-posts for them.' Potentially more useful were the tasks of carrying messages, distributing posters, acting as 'casualties' for air-raid practices, collecting tinfoil and waste paper (3 tons in a single week in October) and gardening. Some Keighley Scouts drilled with the Auxiliary Fire Service and trained in anti-gas measures. And of course, for 'it is a grand pastime', there were sandbags to be filled.

Within the first week of war the Keighley and District Victoria Hospital was protected by 9,000 sandbags (the objective was 20,000), many filled by Boy Scouts. By November they had filled 19,000. By the year-end 110 members of a Civil Nursing Reserve had each gained a minimum of 50 hours' experience on the wards at Victoria Hospital. First-aid posts were supplemented by a saloon motor-coach converted into a 'mobile unit for clearing casualties during air-raids', while even pets were catered for, with their own first-aid post in Alice Street. In the event of raids, vets were also expected to protect the public from 'panic-stricken or gas-contaminated animals'.

On Black Hill, meanwhile, some 900ft above sea-level, overlooking the Aire Valley with eyes and ears attuned towards both Yorkshire and Lancashire the Observer Corps was manning a post twenty-four hours a day for the duration.

Toc H organised a Citizens' Advice Bureau under the auspices of the National Council of Social Service. Its Church Street premises were loaned free

Members of the WVS Hospital Supply Depot photographed in 1941 outside their base in the Conservative Rooms in Cooke Lane. *(Author's collection)*

of rent and rates by Keighley Corporation, while its volunteer advisers included a solicitor, an accountant, a doctor, a chemist and a dentist. In the Conservative Women's Rooms the Keighley Branch of the Soldiers', Sailors' and Airmen's Families Association offered advice and practical help to servicemen's dependants, some of whose problems stemmed from delays in the payment of allowances.

Between early July and the middle of September 1939 the Keighley Section of the Women's Voluntary Services (WVS) enrolled 364 new members; by the end of the year the number would have risen to 573. Their duties ranged from clerical and ARP work to helping with evacuees, driving ambulances, and serving in hospitals and canteens. An initial seventy-eight ladies set up a Hospital Supply Depot in the Conservative Rooms, preparing surgical dressings and raising funds through bring-and-buy sales. When the Princess Royal came to open a new branch of the York County Savings Bank she took the opportunity to visit the WVS and was impressed by what she saw there. She was to visit again in 1945, when the WVS opened a gift shop to collect furniture and household goods for blitzed families in London.

The Keighley Girls' Social Club and the local branch of the National Spinsters' Pension Association were meanwhile busy knitting comforts, the Devonshire Street Women's Friendly Society produced thirty blankets, and seventy women in Bocking, Lees and Cross Roads worked on gloves, scarves and mittens for the crew of 'a war vessel which is somewhere on the high seas under Commander Pigott', husband of a local lady who supplied the wool. Indeed, knitting was blamed for a temporary fall in library book issues, for it seemed as if the entire female population was knitting – the Parish Church Mothers' Union, elderly tenants of the Foster Gardens Bungalows at Guard House and the Women's Patriotic Club, who specialised in hospital bags 'used for keeping any valuables wounded soldiers may have when brought to hospital'. Everywhere church and chapel ladies were 'busy knitting Blankets, Scarves, Helmets and Socks for our own boys and for Soldiers in France'.

The Women's Patriotic Club, a revival from the First World War soon to be renamed the Cravenburn Sewing Party, maintained its momentum through the coming years. By the beginning of 1943 its ladies had produced 5,300 hospital bags and another 530 knitted articles – 120 pullovers, 60 scarves, 57 helmets or balaclavas, 30 pairs of gloves, 13 pairs of mittens, 100 pairs of socks and 100 of hospital slippers. Much of this went to Mrs Amery's Indian Comforts Fund, although one prized member, Mrs Rebecca Sorton, who was on her 200th pair of hand-sewn slippers by 1943, favoured Mrs Churchill's Aid to Russia Fund.

More vitally perhaps, girls as young as 14, mainly from Tyneside, County Durham and Scotland, were being recruited into Keighley's busy textile mills, catching the attention of the national press. 'In a few weeks,' the *Daily Sketch* informed its readers, 'they learn the art of "doffing" – taking full spools from their pegs and replacing them with empty ones'.

Ladies of the WVS Hospital Supply Depot show off some of their work at a bring-and-buy sale at the beginning of the war. *(Keighley News)*

A National Register was being compiled, and identity cards distributed; recipients were asked to memorise their numbers. Food and petrol rationing was in the offing. Faced with imminent complications, shopkeepers founded a Keighley and District Master Bakers' and Confectioners' Association, while a crowded Sunday afternoon meeting of grocers considered the implications of emergency regulations. By November 1939 a Keighley Food Control Committee was posting 56,000 ration books to the registered public.

Land took on an extra value, and 'a remarkably compact yet powerful tractor' attempted to plough up Brow Moor at Haworth. As the war progressed, local farmers would be given official ploughing orders compelling them to turn traditional pasture to growing crops, and barley, oats and corn – not normally seen around Keighley – would be produced.

For agricultural purposes Keighley formed part of a district comprising also Horsforth, Aireborough, Pudsey, Shipley, Bingley and Ilkley. In 1939 its arable production was negligible, but by 1944 some 8,661 acres would be under cultivation. There would be 6,305 milking cows, or one to every 1.35 acres of grassland. The local District Officer of the War Agricultural Committee 'did not know of any other district in almost the whole of England equalling that figure'.

An emotive 'Grow More Food' campaign encouraged allotments, of which Keighley soon laid on 860, though fewer than half of the new plots at Guard House were taken within the first year. Nonetheless, a Leeds University lecturer in horticulture offered practical advice to members of a Keighley Allotment Holders' Association, while a defunct Haworth, Lees and Cross Roads Gardeners' Association was resurrected.

By 1942, spurred on by an even more emotive 'Dig for Victory' slogan, there were some 1,050 Council allotment-holders alone, including women who continued their tenancies after their husbands had been called up. By mid-1943 Keighley Borough had over 2,000 allotment-holders.

Allotments changed the face of many localities. Land acquired by the Town Council for an Aire Valley Road – whose completion lay far in the future – went under cultivation, as did a proposed bowling green at the Oxenhope Recreation Ground, along with an acre of Haworth Recreation Ground and half an acre off View Road. Messrs Robert Clough (Keighley) Ltd contributed an acre and a half at Damems. More than an acre was utilised at Applegarth at Morton Banks, and over two adjoining the Fell Lane County Hospital. Even the sloping green gardens in front of the Charles Edward Sugden's Almshouses at Oakworth were dug up for potatoes.

Enthusiastic pupils of Highfield Council School cultivated more than an acre, one of 437 elementary school gardens throughout the West Riding worked within the first seven months of hostilities. Potatoes formed their main

Pupils of Highfield Council School parade the produce of their early gardening efforts. By March 1940 they had more than an acre of land under cultivation and were enthusiastically 'sowing for victory'. *(Keighley News/Mr C. Edgar)*

crop – by September 1941 they would have produced a total of 10 tons of potatoes, plus two 'fine crops of vegetables and salads'.

Twenty under-10s at Utley Junior Council School dug over their garden – with help from their parents; Eastburn Council School, led by the headmaster, tackled an adjoining field; and Silsden Modern School cultivated a paddock in the Playing Fields. Keighley's Sewage Disposal Committee resolved to grow crops at the Sewage Works but left the choice of seeds to the Borough Engineer. He decided on oats and wheat, and added another 3 acres the following year.

As the first Christmas of the war approached, mothers of Utley Council School pupils packed gifts for the troops. Seasonal parcels from Knowle Park Congregational Chapel were to 'include a good book'; later in 1940 their servicemen were sent booklets containing 'St Mark Gospel, various texts, hymns and prayers and a linen container for each'.

Subscriptions towards a Keighley YMCA hut in France closed at more than £2,000 early in 1940. Machine-tool manufacturers Prince-Smith and Stells Ltd headed the list of donors at £200.

Barely noticed amid wider events, the last of Keighley's Basque children left the Morton Banks camp. Significantly, some had been adopted by British families.

Chapter Three

'To Stick it at all Costs'

Du   uring the course of the Second World War Keighley was to handle
                  some 10,000 official evacuees, plus many more who moved in by
                  private arrangement. On 1 September 1939 – two days before
hostilities and as the Territorial Battalion Headquarters and Headquarters
Company of the 2/6th Duke of Wellington's (West Riding) Regiment were being
mobilised and duly photographed in the Boys' Grammar School playground –
the first evacuees arrived, in the shape of 570 schoolchildren from Bradford.
They came in four special trains (there should actually have been double the
number); then a fleet of buses took them to reception centres in Keighley,
Oakworth, Haworth and Oxenhope for distribution to their new homes.

Bus drivers and policemen near the railway station on 1 September 1939, awaiting the
arrival of Keighley's first evacuees, from Bradford. The sticker in the front window of the
bus says 'Government Evacuation Scheme'. A fleet of such buses took the arriving children
to reception centres in Keighley, Oakworth, Haworth and Oxenhope. *(William Speight/Mr
Trevor M. Leach)*

Each child was issued with two days' rations – a tin of beef, a tin of unsweetened milk and another of sweetened milk, 2lb of chocolate crisps and 1lb of biscuits. The following day another four trains of mothers with children below school age brought Keighley's total of Bradford evacuees up to 1,306.

A substantial number were allocated to Riddlesden, where the Church of England School had to adopt a double-shift system of lessons, from 8 a.m. to noon and from 1 to 5 p.m., and where the evacuees soon adapted a popular song:

South of the Border,
Down Riddlesden way,
We swim in the watter
And laik in the hay.
The apples are lovely,
The plums are O.K.,
South of the Border,
Down Riddlesden way.

The inclusion of apples and plums suggests that a current 'wave of juvenile crime' – largely the raiding of orchards and gardens – was correctly being blamed on the Bradford children!

Bradford is barely 10 miles from Keighley and both are industrial, but the one having been deemed an evacuation and the other a reception area made all the difference. The months of the 'Phoney War' saw a steady flow of children back to Bradford – by mid-October 1939 more than 40 per cent had 'drifted' home – although five Keighley schools opened during the Christmas holidays so that teachers could supervise games or organise trips out for any lonely Bradfordians remaining. At Holycroft Council School, which had admitted twenty-three Bradford and nine private evacuees, teachers attended for the whole of the second week 'to relieve the householders'. Spencer Street Sunday School provided an evacuees' Christmas party, with a film show and community singing.

'Hie you down the street to that lady who has those evacuees to look after, and see if you can do anything for her,' runs a hint as to how Boy Scouts might help the war effort, adding quaintly but not perhaps wholly tongue in cheek: 'She will probably say no; women are like that. The more work they have to do, the happier they are. All the same it is worth the risk and she may be very glad of your offer to help.'

By Christmas 1940 evacuee children's parties were widespread. At one, comprising mainly children from London and Hull, they requested to sing 'On Ilkla Moor Baht 'At'. 'And they sang it lustily enough,' the *Keighley News* tellingly reported, 'though one gained the impression that these "imported"

Battalion Headquarters and Headquarters Company of the 2/6th Duke of Wellington's Regiment pose for local photographer W. Bruce Johnston in the Keighley Boys' Grammar School playground. They were mobilised on 1 September 1939 – two days before war was declared. *(W. Bruce Johnston/Mrs Georgina Eaton)*

children are quieter than the local product, and have an aptitude for being astonishingly quiet during the intervals'.

For a more serious type of evacuee had been arriving since the summer of 1940. The Oakworth Road Institution (Keighley's former Union workhouse) reopened its doors to an initial 120 old people from blitzed London. They included five nonagenarians and twenty octogenarians; the oldest was a 96-year-old woman. Another, French-born Madame Garcier, had been a Court dressmaker. At 92 she was still making dolls' dresses, which were passed on to the Mayoress of Keighley for distribution to organisations holding bring-and-buy sales in aid of comforts funds.

In July forty children arrived from St Peter-in-the-Wood Senior School in occupied Guernsey and were accommodated at Lees and Cross Roads. Lady Butterfield of Cliffe Castle, who had founded a War Emergency Committee for Children of the Fighting Forces, kitted them out with clothes from her friends in America. Occasionally they were allowed to send messages of no more than twenty-five words to their parents courtesy of the Red Cross, though it might be eight months before they received a reply. Their head teacher, Walter C. Brehaut, gave talks to local groups about life in the Channel Islands, and the Guernsey boys' football team at Lees Junior Council School won the Brigg Cup and the Schools' Challenge Shield in 1941.

In October 1940 it was the turn of the entire City of London School for Girls to be evacuated, some 160 pupils plus their teachers. In less than three weeks from being notified of their coming, the Keighley Higher Education Subcommittee managed to find them classroom accommodation in the Junior Technical School, playing fields at the Girls' Grammar School and billets around town – not that this last operation ran altogether smoothly. More than one pupil was to recall a church hall 'rather reminiscent of a cattle market as prospective billeters came in and chose the evacuees they thought would fit into their homes. One heard the various comments they made.'

The City of London School for Girls was a high-class establishment with a syllabus offering a 'religious and virtuous education', including 'the higher branches of literature and all other useful learning'. Its staff-list glittered with Oxford and Cambridge higher degrees and European distinctions. Intending pupils had to produce a recommendation from an alderman or common councilman of the Corporation of London.

'The curriculum has been unchanged by the war,' pluckily stressed the school's prospectus. Keighley, 'near to the Pennine Hills', was considered 'reasonably free from air raids and other disturbances', offering in theory better protection by virtue of its stone-built houses with cellars. The London girls, in their expensive maroon blazers and pinafore dresses, pink-and-white-striped blouses, lisle stockings and velours or Panama hats, brought a distinctive flavour to wartime Keighley. Among their number was future writer and broadcaster Claire Rayner.

Pupils of the City of London School for Girls at a Christmas party in 1940, together with boys from the Junior Technical School. Among the teachers, about the middle of the third row down, sits William Healey, Principal of Keighley Technical College for twenty-four years, but destined to be remembered primarily as Denis Healey's father! *(Mr Roy Parrott)*

To evacuees like these and the many mothers and children escaping the London bombing, life in a northern town must have seemed strange indeed. One, asked for her most striking impressions, picked 'the strange custom of stringing lines of washing across the streets every Monday morning', the 'lackadaisical' approach to daily life, and 'the early hour at which the public 'bus services ceased'!

By the time the City of London School for Girls returned home in 1943, their number had diminished to 120, mainly owing to pupils having reached school-leaving age. On the whole they had enjoyed their stay in Keighley, 'all except the very cold weather'. They were replaced by forty-seven children from 'a South Coast town'.

In 1941 local groups from the Peace Pledge Union, the Fellowship of Reconciliation and the Society of Friends opened the Gledhow Hostel in a large house at Oxenhope – rented for £80 a year – accommodating up to fourteen elderly evacuees who were encouraged, where appropriate, to help with domestic chores. Despite inherent difficulties, a play-reading circle was gamely organised on Monday evenings and poetry appreciation on Fridays.

This project employed conscientious objectors. 'Two of our staff and the Treasurer of our Committee all did a spell of imprisonment during the [first] year', revealed a retrospective survey, 'as a consequence of their refusal to comply with the National Service Regulations'. By the time the Corporation took it over on behalf of the Ministry of Health in 1944, Gledhow had cared for fifty-six elderly people, mostly from London and Hull.

As late as July 1944, when life for some had seemed to be reverting towards normal, a new influx of evacuees arrived from Wimbledon. Ingrow Council School absorbed seventy-nine children, plus a teacher; Eastwood took twenty-three and a teacher, Horkinstone five and Holycroft thirty-four and another teacher. At Ingrow Church of England School, with only forty-nine pupils on its roll, the single Londoner it received must have been a curiosity. Several head teachers' logs tersely record the reason for this displacement of south London schoolchildren: 'Flying bombs.'

By this stage of the war, significantly, evacuees' perceptions of Keighley had changed. One London mother with two young children appreciated the 'advantages of the good air and refreshing sleep' which were 'enhanced by the easy shopping facilities and seeming abundance for commodities found so scarce in my home district'. She was impressed by the courtesy of shop assistants.

Poignantly that August, as part of a London scheme to create hospital space for flying-bomb victims, 144 elderly bedridden patients were evacuated to the

Fell Lane County Hospital. When their train reached Keighley, eighty wardens carried their stretchers to waiting ambulances. One 75-year-old was found to be dying; he passed away at the railway station.

For the local community, of course, evacuees formed only one of many concerns. Although the first eight months of hostilities have been questionably nicknamed the 'Phoney War', they could scarcely have been viewed as such by the families of those who died. Keighley's first casualty, at the very start of 1940, was 20-year-old Private William Smith of the Royal Army Ordnance Corps, fatally injured in France while testing a motorcycle. 'We had a tip-top time,' his last letter home described his festive season. 'Gracie Fields and Jack Payne gave a concert last week. . . . We went to a dance the other night and it was a good laugh, as none of us could dance properly in our boots.'

Engine-room artificer John Wilkinson was reported missing aboard the submarine *Starfish*, sunk in the Heligoland Bight, but survived as a prisoner of war. Seamen Edward Slater and George Sanderson went down with HMS *Daring*.

In March 1940 Mrs Maud Marks, a middle-aged mother whose children had grown up, volunteered for service with the Salvation Army in France, where her usefulness far transcended the serving of tea and buns to the troops, as her autograph album from that April attests: 'Every time you scan this little book, think of Alex and Geoff, who greatly appreciated your many kindnesses and cheerful smile' . . . 'Keep your face towards the sunshine and the shadows will fall behind you. In memory of many laughs and smiles.' But the mood changed abruptly in the penultimate week of May. A Salvation Army Major drove Mrs Marks's party of seven women and three men in a covered wagon through the confusion of retreat, repeatedly bombed, along roads clogged with refugees. One of their younger workers 'went a bit mental'. They were still in France days after the Dunkirk evacuation, in the middle of June.

When Mrs Marks providentially arrived back in Keighley, the Salvation Army ladies requested a talk on her adventures. She was no public speaker, so she bought a cheap exercise-book and wrote down her experiences, which seem all the more vivid because of their brevity and absence of punctuation:

> We escaped to St Nazaire where we waited in a field and was bombed all night we were in slip trenches and then we marched to the docks about 100 of us noncombatants and a ship a Polish one with all Polish waiters brought us to Plymouth with about 4,000 troops aboard as well.

The local paper baldly said she had been 'helping at one of these "Army" huts'!

Life became much more tense following the Fall of France. Holidays for ARP staff and Civil Defence volunteers were suspended. Under War Office orders, road blocks went up on Keighley's main approaches from Skipton and

Halifax. The Town Council, grappling with the escalating problem of replacing its called-up male employees, took time to discuss the protection of the Town Hall windows, deciding to have them covered with adhesive net and varnished on the inside. Councillors were instructed 'to exercise the strictest economy in the use of paper'. The Chief Librarian reported a slump in his supply of free magazines, and even the Ministry of Information's own weekly *Noteworthy* bulletin, distributed to senior schools and members of the Elementary Education Subcommittee, ceased publication.

There was talk of an enemy 'parachute menace' as prelude to an invasion. 'Anyone seeing parachute troops landing in this country', went one instruction, 'should immediately tell the police'. Fears of a 'Fifth Column' appeared not to be unfounded. In June Stanley Noel Jenkinson of Manningham, Bradford, ARP organiser for the Keighley, Bingley, Shipley and Denholme Joint Area, was detained under 'the Home Secretary's warrant'. The last the local public knew of him was his being 'removed under guard from Keighley "for detention elsewhere"'. The reason for his detention (which probably should not have been reported at the time) was never explained, though a possible clue may lie

Cricketer Eddie Paynter, being invested with his Keighley Stickers' Club badge in July 1940, during the interval of a match against Bingley. The clergyman on the right was the Revd John Nicholson Balmer of Devonshire Street Congregational Chapel, who had been chairman of a Yorkshire Committee for Spanish Relief. *(Keighley News/Keighley Reference Library)*

This children's stall at Stockbridge raised £8 7s for the Spitfire–Hurricane Fund. Judging by the apparent quality of the pictures and bric-à-brac, there seems in retrospect to have been some bargains. (*Keighley News/Mrs D. Bottomley*)

in his alleged credentials of having worked in intelligence during the First World War and having spent some time in Germany afterwards.

Place-names disappeared under a sweeping decree: 'No person shall display or cause or permit to be displayed any sign which affords any indication of the

name of, or the situation of, or the direction of, or the distance to any place.'
The word 'Keighley' was duly painted out from the sides of Corporation
vehicles, while at the bottom of Haworth main street an indicator of Brontë
sites, unveiled for the 1937 Coronation, went into storage for the duration, lest
it offer clues to literary German paratroopers.

The public responded meanwhile by joining the Local Defence Volunteer
Corps, handing in their aluminium pans and kettles, and launching a morale-

boosting trail-blazer in the shape of the Keighley Stickers' Club. This simple way to help 'defeat defeatism' (as they phrased it) emerged from one of the many patriotic meetings held during War Effort Week in July. Out of a well-meaning welter of declarations (facing the future with courage and determination, encouraging public spirit and maintaining morale, establishing a bond of comradeship in service and loyalty) the Stickers' Club was born. Nothing could have been simpler. Members paid a penny, for which they received a badge shaped like a letter 'S' and signed a card bearing the Club rules: 'To stick it at all costs, whatever the enemy do; to obey the advice and instructions of the government, and to wear the badge.'

The Stickers' Club was run by a typical town committee – an ex-mayor, one or two textile men, a journalist and a Congregational minister, the Mayor's mace-bearer. The Chief Librarian distributed the badges, and the Honorary Treasurer worked at Barclay's Bank. Not that raising money was their intention: the aim – rather more grandly phrased than on the membership card – was solely 'to bring civilians together and to provide them with a visible sign of their unity and complete participation in the national effort to win the war'. It was felt that housewives and munition workers would especially want to be Stickers.

The Stickers' Club was appropriately launched during War Effort Week, in which thirty-seven open-air meetings were held in Keighley. Broadcaster Professor John Hilton visited under the auspices of the Ministry of Information and spoke in the Municipal Hall. People stood all down the aisles, and his speech was relayed to an adjoining hall and the Town Hall Square outside ('I go pretty extensively about this country and talk in heart-to-heart talks with soldiers and civilians, and everywhere I find the note of determination that we will see this thing through!'). Professor Hilton was publicly enrolled as Sticker No. 1.

Sticker No. 2 was Eddie Paynter, the England and Lancashire cricketer then playing for Keighley. He was invested with his 'S' badge during the interval of a match against Bingley, and went on to score 45 in an innings lasting an hour and a quarter.

Within days the Keighley Stickers' Club had enrolled more than 2,000 members, and its committee had run out of badges. Some wanted 'a more permanent form of badge at a slightly higher charge to cover the extra cost', so 'a neat brooch-badge', suitable for both men and women, was produced costing 3*d*. Existing members who had lost their original badges or who preferred the superior model could buy them on showing their membership cards, 'duly signed', to 'an authorised enrolling member'. In little over a fortnight there were 4,000 Keighley Stickers.

The fame of this modest little enterprise spread. Enquiries arrived from Morecambe, Manchester and Colwyn Bay. By August Worthing, to which a Keighley resident had moved, was forming its own Club, the Keighley

This very homely stall in Moss Street raised £2 11s for the Spitfire–Hurricane Fund. The close-knit nature of the community is epitomised by the youngsters, who included three Cannons, three Pearsons, three Andersons, three Taylors, two Conleys, two Hewlitts and two Meagans. *(Keighley News/Mr D. Cannon)*

committee sending good wishes to its south coast fellow-Stickers. Even a national Stickers' Club was suggested.

Late in August Keighley's MP, H.B. Lees-Smith, joined (a little tardily, one feels). By September a Bradford Club was enrolling members, and there were nearly 7,000 Keighley Stickers. The committee had acquired some strirrup-pumps for allocation to parties of Stickers who were prepared to form themselves into Strirrup-pump Groups. Another idea involved 'working groups among neighbour members', making garments and comforts for the WVS. Members were also being asked to contribute to the Lord Mayor of London's Air Raid Fund.

But the Keighley Stickers' Club itself was already running out of steam. Recruitment faltered through another shortage of badges and membership cards. The tone of the war was changing. Many Stickers were engaged in other, more active, forms of war work. The Chief Librarian took on a more onerous duty than the distribution of badges, as organising secretary of a local Spitfire–Hurricane Fund. The Stickers' Club had provided a simple, popular boost to morale at a time of very special need. Now, as the Second World War moved on, we were assuredly sticking it.

The Spitfire–Hurricane Fund epitomised, later that summer and autumn, a determined community spirit as Keighley helped replace aircraft losses in the Battle of Britain through a welter of money-raising activities such as concerts, dances, whist drives, garden parties, bring-and-buy sales, and cinema and door-to-door collections. Drawings of aeroplanes, each 15ft by 10ft, were

Audience and performers at an outdoor concert in Gladstone Street in 1940, when songs, dances, recitations and a short play performed by four young girls raised 15s 6d for the Spitfire–Hurricane Fund. *(Keighley News/Mrs Mary Lyness)*

ranged round the Town Hall Square, the public being invited to fill in the outlines with coins. Drinkers in one Keighley hotel dipped over 500 pennies in beer and stuck them to a mirror! Ironically, the sale of German propaganda leaflets (people collected them as souvenirs) raised £6 10s. At Riddlesden a barrel-organ and a mile of pennies netted £11 11s 7½d.

Children played a prominent part in fund-raising. Four girls in Gladstone Street, aged between 10 and 13, put on a little open-air concert and collected

15s 6d from neighbours; one of their mothers added a 'pie tea' which brought in another 13s. A roadside bric-à-brac stall at Stockbridge raised £8 7s; another in Hainworth Road £6 10s, nearly a third of which came from 'an autographed cover, which bore the names, worked in silk, of those who had paid 3d each for the privilege'. Moss Street children collected £2 11s by selling ornaments, pictures and home produce. Many juvenile fund-raisers were officially photographed presenting their contributions to Mayor J.W. Wardle.

Samples from the Fund's exhaustive lists of donors and collecting-boxes portray the community flavour of this appeal:

Children played a prominent part in Spitfire–Hurricane Fund-raising, many being photographed presenting their contributions to Mayor J.W. Wardle. Here is young Thelma Wright handing over £5 5s which she had raised by selling scent bags. *(Keighley News/Author's collection)*

Employees of Timothy Hird and Sons, Ltd., Acres and Knowle Mills. Boxes 125 and 126. £4 8s 9½d . . .

Beaconsfield Club. Box 74. 14s 3d . . .

G. Hunt (Comedian) c/o Grapes Inn. 6s . . .

Mrs Doris Naylor, Cushion Raffle. 12s . . .

Salts (Saltaire) Ltd. and their operatives and Staff. £150 0s 0d . . .

Public Library. £1 1s 3d . . .

Streamline Taxis. £1 0s 6d . . .

Oxenhope House to House Collection per Misses M. and B. Denby. £4 16s 0d . . .

The White Horse Inn, Ingrow. Box 339. 7½d . . .

Penny a week from a few friends. £1 0s 0d . . .

Lund Park Veterans. £20 0s 0d . . .

Stanbury Ladies Knitting Circle per Miss Metcalfe. £5 0s 2d . . .

Staff at Keighley Corporation Baths. £2 12s 1d . . .

Bogthorn Air Raid Shelter Ladies Effort. £11 0s 0d . . .

At work on the Keighley and District Spitfire. Obviously this was a public relations view, centred on the Borough coat-of-arms on the aircraft's fuselage. *(Keighley Reference Library)*

By November 1940 Keighley's total contribution to the national Spitfire–Hurricane Fund amounted to £11,600, which paid for both a Spitfire and a Hurricane and still left something over for the RAF Benevolent Fund. Engineers Dean, Smith and Grace Ltd also financed their own Spitfire.

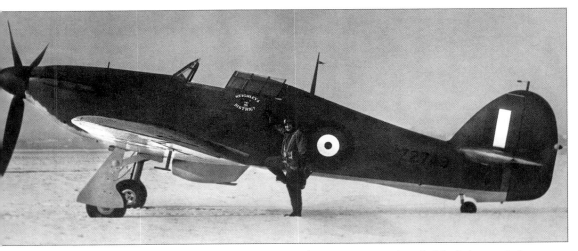

The Keighley and District Hurricane. The Borough crest appears just behind the cockpit. *(Keighley Reference Library)*

In the spirit of the summer of 1940, staff of the Keighley–West Yorkshire Bus Services undergo arms drill outside their garage at Anvil Street. Not quite all of them seem to be taking the exercise too seriously! *(Author's collection)*

More modestly at the Rectory, meanwhile, Mrs Hood (who incidentally was Patuffa Kennedy-Fraser, daughter of the composer of 'Songs of the Hebrides') was appealing for books to send out to the Forces in Iceland, where her husband, the Revd Canon J.C.F. Hood, was serving as Chaplain-in-Chief. The first consignment included a hundred novels collected by Girl Guides. 'Two huge parcels of books just arrived,' the Rector wrote home appreciatively. 'Just the right sort.'

At a practical level, from early summer onwards the Home Guard (HG) – known for their first couple of months as the Local Defence Volunteer (LDV) Corps – enrolled with enthusiasm, more than 35,000 men joining in the West Riding alone during the first ten days. They were as young as 17 and as old as 65. Such were the exigencies of the period that, to begin with, they could expect 'no large measure of drill, and there was no time for rifle practice'; since rifles were in short supply, the latter was largely academic anyway. All some recruits got was an LDV armlet, exchanged for an HG armlet that July, when the Volunteers became the Home Guard.

Some officers and NCOs of the Keighley Home Guard, the majority of whom are wearing First World War medals. Major John Edwin Tillotson, DSO, MC, sits in the centre. In civilian life he was chief salesman for brewers Timothy Taylor and Co. Ltd, and a notable breeder of budgerigars. Seated third from the left is Alderman Ernest Whalley, a branch manager for the Keighley Industrial Co-operative Society Ltd, who had been mayor in 1933–4. Lieutenant Horace S. Reynolds, sitting second from the left, would be awarded the British Empire Medal in 1955 for services to the Corporation Gas Department. *(William Speight/Mr S. Reynolds)*

Once issued with rifles, but not ammunition, some over-eager personnel at nearby Bingley had to be ordered to stop making themselves dummy rounds out of spent cases and 'wood shaped with a pencil sharpener', which jammed and damaged the rifle mechanism!

Even at such a time of national emergency, local government protocol was observed. The Local Defence Volunteers had to apply to the Elementary School Buildings and Caretakers' Subcommittee for permission to drill on the

Members of the Keighley Home Guard practise the prone firing position. This was probably their miniature rifle team in 1941, formed 'to stimulate interest in rifle shooting'. They entered competitions with other units, including Regulars. *(Keighley Reference Library)*

Members of the Keighley Home Guard, in rather light-hearted mood, in a defensive position which, judging by the spades, they have just built. *(Author's collection)*

playground at Eastwood Council School. When later the Home Guard wanted 'to dig a few trenches in order to carry out exercises' in the Parkwood Recreation Ground, these had to be in a position approved by the Parks Superintendent. They had to pay, albeit at a reduced rate, for the use of the Baths Hall for lectures on 'Defensive Schemes' and 'Fires Caused by Incendiary Bombs'. At any rate, the Gas Committee allowed them the 'occasional' use of their 'Commer' motor wagon.

Posterity has tended to be less than just to the Home Guard, so often recalled in humorous vein. In reality, many were ex-servicemen with experience in the First World War and even the Boer War. Major John Edwin Tillotson of the Keighley Home Guard had been, as a 19-year-old Second Lieutenant in 1918, one of the youngest winners of the Distinguished Service Order (DSO); he also held the Military Cross (MC), as did Major Norman Feather. Most formal group portraits include a proportion of First World War ribbons. Forty-five early recruits from Haworth were members of the British Legion.

Of course, the Home Guard were originally intended to deal, not with enemy panzer divisions, but with the paratroopers expected to precede a full-scale invasion. The reality of routine service, devoid of such questionable excitement, must have seemed an anticlimax. 'Very quiet morning with hang-dog atmosphere,' noted one log after an armed night watch, 'which makes one long to cry there will always be an England, to hell with the Nazis. Nothing doing at all.'

At least they were treated to occasional mock action. One sunny Sunday morning in 1941 Keighley became the centre of an exercise in which the Home Guard fought off Regulars masquerading as German paratroopers and saboteurs – one was dressed as a woman and another as a policeman on a bicycle! Careless members of the public, out for a stroll without their gas masks or identity cards, found themselves 'inconvenienced' by tear gas or rounded up as suspects. Perhaps they could draw solace from a useful lesson and the fact that 'most of the attacks on public utility services were broken up and the vital points kept safe from damage'.

By 1942 the emphasis had shifted. One exercise graphically pretended 'that the enemy was sweeping down from a bridgehead it had established in the north-east, and was moving towards the industrial regions, having captured the stronghold of Skipton'. The resulting attacks involved the Home Guard in conjunction with police, air-raid wardens, ambulance and first-aid parties, demolition squads and the National Fire Service. There was what the local press described as 'fierce street fighting', in which the Home Guard by now enjoyed plenty of blanks for their 'rifles, machine-guns and tommy-guns'.

Chapter Four

'Don't Turn away the Camderonians!'

Avariety of Regular Army units was stationed in and around Keighley at
various times – elements of the Duke of Wellington's (West Riding)
Regiment and the Sherwood Foresters; the Royal Artillery and the
Royal Armoured Corps; the Royal Ulster Rifles, the Manchester Regiment, the
Durham Light Infantry and the Cameronians or Scottish Rifles – bringing an
entire new plethora of manners and accents into the community. Some of these
young men met local girls and returned after the war.

The initial impression of one soldier from London, having no idea where he
was and first glimpsing Keighley's prominent Mechanics' Institute clock-tower
on a rainy grey dawn, was 'I've come to a university town!' Notwithstanding his
mistake, after 1945 he would spend the rest of his life here.

The Pennine terrain was not always appropriate for military vehicles. Five
soldiers were injured, one seriously, when their Bren-gun carrier got out of
control down Brow Top Road at Haworth, spectacularly crossing Hebden
Road, mounting the pavement, crashing through a gap made by a previous
accident, dropping to a lower level, careering over a pile of stones and hitting a
house. The housewife, in her adjacent kitchen, had to be treated for shock.

Troops were billeted in factories and the Temperance Hall, which boasted
such recreational amenities as a canteen, four billiard tables and a Services'
library accumulated by asking the public to donate books, an expedient that
brought in the complete works of Shakespeare, the mysteries of Euclid and
dictionaries, the latter proving useful for a popular pastime of doing crossword
puzzles. 'We're all reight here,' remarked a soldier from Bradford. 'I could stop
i' Keighley for t'rest of t'war.'

Keighley Toc H opened a Talbot House Service Club in Holker Street,
'where troops could gather and wheβre a soldier could meet his wife or
sweetheart'. Spiritual needs were discreetly provided for by a chapel tucked
away on the top floor. The Club's supply of some 35,000 cigarettes a month
offers a clue both to the number of troops using it and to their smoking habits;

it was also 'well supplied with chocolates' before they were rationed, and 'a reasonable choice of food'. In 1942 Toc H headquarters reduced the cigarettes to 2,800 a month, but 'I can assure you', the Honorary Secretary told his Management Committee, 'that this position is not being accepted, and that every possible avenue and pressure is being explored to rectify it.'

Servicemen were allowed to attend the School of Art and Crafts without paying fees and later the Technical College gymnasium out of school hours. Eventually Morton was authorised to have street lights near the church, the post office, the Co-operative stores and the Busfeild Arms on the grounds of 'numerous complaints of soldiers stationed in the district losing their way at night'.

As early as October 1939 soldiers stationed in the town – the *Keighley News* was careful not to divulge what unit they represented, but the Town Council Institute Buildings Subcommittee identified them as the 2/6th Battalion Duke of Wellington's Regiment (TA), as a year later they would similarly identify the 143rd AA 'Z' Battery RA – were giving concerts in the Municipal Hall, featuring such turns as a brass quartet and accordion solos, two crooners and a comic wrestling match between the 'Lawkholme Kid' and the 'Demon Barber'.

During severe winter weather men of the 14th Battalion the Sherwood Foresters helped with snow removal, in appreciation of which the Town Council donated £35 to their Regimental Institute. When they left early in 1941 their commanding officer assured the Mayor that Keighley had been 'quite the happiest station in which we have served'. The Mayor reciprocated with a silver-plated bugle inscribed with the Borough coat-of-arms in appreciation of the 'excellent relationship between Keighley and officers and men of the Sherwood Foresters'.

On Christmas Day 1943 twenty-six soldiers who had saved up their sweets ration for seven weeks entertained thirty-five children of prisoners of war to a party of jellies, cakes and chocolates. After games and the obligatory community singing the children were taken home in taxis.

Some details not reported at the time surfaced later on. In 1944 the local paper received a letter from a Heavy Anti-Aircraft Regiment in South-East Asia Command, some of whose personnel waxed nostalgic over the ten weeks they had been billeted in Keighley in 1941. They recalled 'memories of your most beautiful countryside, and what you people of Keighley did for us in the way of individual entertainment', vividly describing their departure: 'The station at midnight was packed with cheering crowds, and our send-off was a great memory, hundreds of gifts, embraces, and handshakes.' 'Some of us boys have sweethearts there,' they added significantly, 'others wives . . .'

Not that relations were invariably rosy, according to a field general court-martial in 1942 on two men from the Duke of Wellington's Regiment and two from a searchlight unit of the Royal Artillery accused of assaulting a sergeant of the Royal Armoured Corps in the Victoria Hotel where, in the colloquial words

This was 'C' Company, 9th Battalion the Cameronians or Scottish Rifles, photographed in Victoria Park in March 1944, shortly before leaving for Hove in preparation for the Normandy landings. The back of this original print was covered with autographs and such comments as 'E.J. Stevens (a wee lad from London)', 'T. Beard (known to the Boys as Spike)', 'Nobby (from 'Lambeth Walk', a Cockney Boy)' and 'Cpl Watkinson (We'll meet again – Hare & Hounds)'. *(Keighley Reference Library)*

of a waiter, soldiers and civilians had 'three do's' at fighting. A woman witness said 'the place was in an uproar'. Their defending officer was probably correct in suggesting that 'it was a brawl in a public-house in which a large number of people were concerned; everybody was hitting everybody and nobody definitely'. Nonetheless the sergeant spent twelve days in hospital.

The Royal Army Service Corps was billeted at Haworth, where a 'very successful Canteen, with a full programme of entertainment etc.' was run by a Haworth HM Forces Welfare Committee. When billeting was discontinued this 'turned its attention to the entertainment and care of wounded soldiers from the Hospitals at Bradford and Horsforth'. In 1944 two motor-coaches of soldiers

from St Luke's Hospital, Bradford, were shown the Brontë moors (those who were able had a short walk) and given tea and a concert in the Bridgehouse Sunday School. 'Cigarettes in abundance' were supplied, and the park gardener decorated the tables with dahlias. When the Royal Army Medical Corps left Sutton-in-Craven in 1943 the vicar conducted a farewell service, observing that 'the officers and men came among them as strangers and left as friends'.

The Cameronians especially made their mark. To this day elderly Keighley women who were then girls can still sing home-made songs about the Cameronians:

> Don't turn away the Cameronians,
> They will be needed by and by.
> Every one of the Cameronians
> Is ready to do or die.
> (I don't think!)

> Don't turn away the Cameronians,
> Better than the Navy on the sea.
> If it wasn't for the Cameronians
> Where would Old England be?
> (Buggered if I know!) . . .

'The Cameronians were stationed in Pilgrim's Mill at East Parade,' one 1940s girl remembers. 'Also they had their own band and used to play for dances at the Baths Hall.'

The 9th Battalion the Cameronians arrived in Keighley in 1943 and left, in preparation for the Normandy landings, in April 1944 – long enough to become established in the town. Their Pipe Major had appeared in Alexander Korda's pre-war film *The Drum*, and they fielded a good football team, which included several former professionals. Battalion sports were held in Victoria Park. When one of their carriers, driving down Low Street in wintry conditions, skidded into the window of a furnishing store, its proprietor put up a good-humoured notice saying 'The Army Like Our Furniture! Why Not You?'

Although it included soldiers who had served in India on the North-West Frontier in the 1930s, the 9th Battalion while in Keighley had never been in action as a unit. During the last eleven months of the war in Europe, its official history records – out of a total fighting strength of 700 – 259 killed in action, 67 died of wounds, and 19 other deaths. Such casualties, although including replacements over and above the original 700, tell their own story. 'This', as one old Cameronian comments, 'is the price of freedom'.

The Cameronians – including their padre – enjoy a donkey and pony gymkhana by the Lawkholme sports fields. *(Keighley Reference Library)*

Another unit, strictly local but whose purpose demonstrated that the war was never quite as far away as it may sometimes have seemed, was the Observer Corps (which gained its 'Royal' prefix in 1941). Keighley's Black Hill post was one of a cluster of four – the others were at Beamsley, Cowling and Gargrave – 'with an open circuit so that everyone could hear as aircraft passed overhead'. These were manned twenty-four hours a day throughout the war. Observer volunteers served twelve hours a week fulfilling a rota whereby at least two members were on duty at any one time, with a basic task of recognising and tracking aircraft and relaying information to headquarters. By the end of the war an experienced Observer could quickly identify up to 140 different types.

Years later Eric Binns, one of two full-time Observers on the Black Hill post, wrote down his memories. 'We often had to dig our way in and out of the post through drifts of snow,' he remembered, 'and when you were on duty from 10 p.m. to 10 a.m. it was pretty rough going at times'. But he could hardly recall anybody missing duty on account of bad weather.

The conditions in 1939 were primitive, comprising simply a tent with 'a line run down to the police station', but the 'Phoney War' period provided an opportunity for improvement, and the Black Hill post became the envy of its cluster. It graduated to a wooden building. An optician Observer supplied a fixed telescope of 'immense range', which on one occasion later in the war enabled the post to see a V2 rocket (code-named 'Spiral' because they went up corkscrew fashion) shortly after being launched in Holland. It was 360 miles away and nearly 60 miles high.

The Black Hill post was attuned towards both Yorkshire and Lancashire. 'When they bombed Hull and Liverpool at the same time,' wrote Observer Binns, 'I can recall seeing the "chandelier" flares dropping down. This on both coasts. They were like a lighted-up house with many windows lit.'

War came very close indeed 'when they bombed Bradford' and 'the Junkers 88s had several run-ins before they dropped their bombs and they turned just about over our Post and one could see the red flames from the exhausts of the enemy aircraft'. By then, Black Hill had been issued with one loaded rifle!

Observer William Ward volunteered to accompany the D-Day invasion forces as an aircraft identifier. Late in 1944 a V1 missile destined for Sowerby Bridge passed over the Black Hill post. 'The engine stopped,' recalled the Head Observer. 'We thought the bomb was coming down.'

'We had several crashes,' Observer Binns tersely recorded events kept quiet at the time.

One at Nab End . . . A wing of a Wellington broke off near Bradley – that crashed. A Whitley crashed at Silsden. Another Whitley crashed on Ilkley

The Royal Observer Corps at their Black Hill post. *(Keighley Reference Library)*

Moor. They thought they were over the sea, because they threw out their dinghies. Another bomber crashed near Oakworth. It was a terrible night and although only a few miles away nobody heard anything on the post. A Miles Master aircraft came down on Keighley Golf Course. It was damaged – they cleverly put it on a canal boat and took it back to its base. . . .

Not far away, at Whitley Head above Steeton, Robert Smith Williams of the West Riding Special Constabulary had similar concerns. Wounded during the First World War and now caretaker at Steeton Council School and serving on both the Skipton Rural and the Steeton-with-Eastburn Parish Councils, Special Constable Williams took his duties very seriously, and his notebook throws light on a subject where the strictest censorship prevailed.

He logged his first 'siren raid warning' on 20 June 1940, and his last on 17 March 1945. In between he had noted a total of sixty-one, not counting other alarms for which the sirens had not sounded. The majority of Steeton's air-raid warnings came between August and October 1940 and between March and June 1941. Most were at night. They could last for a few minutes or for many hours. Special Constable Williams developed an ear for sirens. One, towards Cowling, he found very confusing. Instead of warbling and wailing, this emitted 'short blasts on the same note', and he thought it might be mistaken for the 'All Clear'. Reassuringly, when a new siren at the Royal Ordnance Factory at Steeton went into action for the first time on 12 March 1941 it 'sounded alright'.

Like Observer Binns, Special Constable Williams was awake during 31 August/1 September 1940, when Bradford was bombed, though he did not know what he was describing when he noted the night's events:

Great aerial activity tonight from 10.15 p.m. onwards. Very clear night, slight Westerly wind. Sound of explosions heard very clear at 11.35 p.m and 11.40 p.m. and again at 1 o'clock a.m. in a Westerly direction. Big glare in sky in southeasterly direction at 10.15 p.m. to about 12 o'clock p.m. Turned in at 3 a.m.

As the first part of this entry shows, Special Constable Williams was aware of both Lancashire and Yorkshire directions. He would make this point again on 3/4 May 1941, the night Double Summer Time came into force and an air-raid warning lasted for nearly five hours:

Moonlight night and quite a stream of aircraft passed over and seemed to be making towards Merseyside. Flashes in sky also pointed to it being in this area. Cold frosty night.

His notebook drops some tantalising hints, as on the night of 1 September 1942, when there was no siren 'but a plane going down the valley dropped 2 flares in the direction of Robin Hood and another pair in the direction of Morton. Nothing further happened.' Or a short morning raid on 21 December 1940, when incendiary bombs were dropped on Haworth Moor. Observer Binns also gave an undated recollection of incendiaries – 'one lot started at Haworth and finished up at Bingley. It burnt a garage and car out.'

There were other, more serious, episodes. Special Constable Williams's ignorance, at the time of writing, of the night's events adds poignancy to 4/5 May 1941, when a German bomber crashed on Idle, near Bradford, killing several residents: 'Moonlight night and plenty of planes about, part gunfire could be heard. Two very loud explosions at 12.15 to 12.30 sounded fairly local.'

Or 22 March 1943, when a Mosquito crashed at White Crag, Silsden:

No sirens, but I saw lights in the sky followed by dull thuds. Afterwards the sky was lit up by a big red glare, one or two planes could be heard in the distance. Direction N.E. Wind N.E. Moon overcast. Time 8.45 approx. Fire out 9.25 approx.

For communities not directly scarred by war, it was the aircraft crashes that brought the reality home most horribly. Here is the statement of an 18-year-old member of the Home Guard who happened to be first on the scene of a crash near Hayhills Farm, above Silsden, on 28 August 1940:

On the night of 28.8.40, W. Dobson, R. Fort and myself were on duty at the Silsden Reservoir Post.

A 'plane passed over flying in a westerly direction at 23.00 hours, flew back again, circled a few times and crashed at approximately 23.07 hours about 500 yards away. We immediately ran towards the 'plane which was burning furiously and were about 50 yards away when there were two explosions, which I thought were exploding petrol tanks.

Dobson and myself were first on the scene and managed to get through the petrol blazing on the ground to one flyer who was lying near the trailing edge of the starboard wing, by the rear gun turret which had apparently broken off on impact. I sent Fort back to the reservoir to telephone Major Driver.

Ammunition was continually exploding but the flyer was too heavy for us to carry and we did not drag him away because of possible internal injuries. He was badly burned about the face and hands, but we could do nothing except try to clean the slight cuts with a field dressing. He appeared to be conscious, but we could get no intelligible replies as to whether there were any more still in the 'plane, or whether they were carrying any bombs. He spoke vaguely about Dishforth, Driffield and Leeming Aerodromes. . . . This was the first intimation we had that it was a British 'plane.

Two farmers and a woman who had meanwhile arrived assisted us in carrying the gunner away from the aircraft which was now distinguishable as a bomber. People then began to appear from all sides and we had considerable difficulty in keeping them away from the machine. I sent one civilian who had a motor cycle back to show the Ambulance etc. the nearest way, as from a distance it was not clear which road was nearest to the accident.

About this time the remainder of 'B' Section arrived from the Cringles and Moorcock posts.

The fire was by this time abating and a Silsden R.A.F. Flight-Sergeant made an inspection and confirmed that no bombs were being carried. The Home Guard threw a cordon round the aircraft and later the four bodies of the remainder of the crew were found.

The Home Guard were relieved about 03.00 hours by the Military.

The aircraft was an Armstrong-Whitworth Whitley IV, carrying a crew of five.

We have quoted this statement at length not simply for its graphic details – the crashing Whitley bomber also killed a horse – but because of the mature performance of the 18-year-old Home Guard private, who even fifty years later preferred to remain unidentified. The aircraft, which had been on a training flight from Leeming airfield, had been flown by Sergeant-Pilot Norman Kelvin Bott, who was a fortnight short of his twenty-first birthday. Sergeant Leonard Geoffrey Smalley, the rear gunner and sole survivor from a crew of five, was 19.

Sergeant-Pilot Bott was from Leicester and had joined the RAFVR on the outbreak of war. His twenty-first birthday cake had been baked, and his traditional gold watch bought. His parents sent his cake to the children's ward at Leicester Royal Infirmary.

Sergeant Smalley, from March in Cambridgeshire, was burned on the face, head, back and hands; he also suffered a bruised kidney and broken fingers. He recuperated in Keighley Victoria Hospital, where he insisted on wearing his flying-boots along with his pyjamas and dressing-gown. Later he flew as a wireless-operator, was shot down over Holland and spent three and a half years as a prisoner of war.

'It should be known', Sergeant-Pilot Bott's sister echoes the old Cameronian quoted earlier, 'just how our young men gave their lives for us to enjoy freedom.'

The Hayhills Farm crash illustrates an especially depressing feature, for the fire and explosions had naturally roused 'great excitement' in the area. 'There was a mass exodus by the locals,' one forthright resident recalled, 'who blocked the narrow farm lane and made it impossible for the firefighting tenders and the ambulances to get through'. The Silsden Fire Brigade negotiated five fields to reach the scene. The same witness remembered the site 'swarming with children' by first light following the Mosquito crash in 1943:

> Children were seen coming away from the crash with their pockets crammed with live ammunition picked up off the moor. I distinctly remember seeing one child of about ten deliberately throwing 20mm cannon shells against a wall trying to make them explode. One more knowledgeable child thrust them nose first into the cracks in the dry stone wall and was pelting the detonator end with stones. There was a great rounding up by the police and hundreds of rounds of both cannon shells and machine-gun ammunition were recovered. One round must have got through because it was thrown on the fire at home by a boy and the resultant explosion cost his father an eye.

Similarly, after the crash of a Wellington bomber near Tewitt Hall, above Oakworth, at the beginning of 1944 – its Canadian crew of six all died – 'the wreckage was plundered for souvenirs by members of the public' early next morning. When another Wellington came down across the main Skipton road near Bradley Lane End one midday in 1943, killing its crew of six Poles, blazing fiercely and setting the vegetation alight along the Leeds and Liverpool Canal, 'a considerable number of spectators appeared from goodness knows where' and had to be kept back by the Home Guard.

Fortunately it was sometimes possible to manage the aftermath of an accident with decorum, like this forgotten forced landing of 1944 buried in the Police Incidents Register at Keighley:

P.C. 883 Myers reports receiving information at 12 noon, 24.8.44 from P.C.
Shepherd, of Glusburn, Skipton Division that an aircraft had made a forced
landing at 11.10 a.m. this date, in a field known as High Pasture, New Hall
Farm, Sutton-in-Craven.

P.C. 883 Myers immediately went to the scene & found Insp. Driver,
P.S. 1132 Drury & P.C. Shepherd present. He found that a Fairy Swordfish
Biplane No. H.S. 346 carrying Pilot Acting Sub. Lt. No. 153053 Brierley,
R.N.V.R., Observer Sub. Lt. Roy Hillier, R.N.A.S. & Air Gunner &
Telegraphist No. J.X. 453916 had been compelled to make a forced landing
owing to engine trouble. There were no injuries & no fire. Plane extensively
damaged. Pilot informed his base by Telephone. Military Guard provided by
the Pioneer Corps of Skipton.

What could have been a serious disaster of a different kind occurred at
Steeton railway station at a quarter to five on the morning of 11 October 1943,
when the Leeds to Edinburgh express collided with a freight train being
shunted into a siding. Wreckage was strewn along 200 yards of track and over
the level crossing, blocking the road between Steeton and Silsden. The express
engine toppled on its side, its carriages overturned or derailed. Ten freight
waggons were smashed, two ending up in the stationmaster's garden, scattering
sacks of cattle-cake intended for Skipton.

Amazingly, although the Scottish express had been carrying some 200
passengers, there were no fatalities and only four were briefly detained in
Keighley Victoria Hospital. Engine-driver John Bonner, who had been driving
since 1908 without experiencing any previous accident, escaped serious injury
by clinging to a rail in his cab. Mrs Little, the Steeton stationmaster's wife, did
the best she could for the shocked and temporarily stranded passengers. 'Out
of her small ration of tea, sugar, and milk,' the press noted in a period detail,
'she made as many cups of tea as possible'.

Occasional and slightly less dramatic alarms included the summer afternoon
in 1941 when a barrage balloon, which had broken loose from its moorings,
floated across the district, trailing a cable which fouled a number of overhead
lines and disabled Keighley's electricity for nearly an hour. The cable then
touched a pylon at Frizinghall and the balloon burst into flames, injuring three
children, including twin brothers, one hit on the head by 'an electrified cable'
and the other treated for burns.

Barrage balloons tend to remain a relatively unsung feature of the Home
Front, but the rigours of a balloon site are vividly painted in a letter home from
a Keighley aircraftman serving over the Lancashire border on the Accrington
barrage protecting an aircraft factory (whence Keighley's errant balloon may

This was the overturned Leeds–Edinburgh express at Steeton station on 11 October 1943. Amazingly, considering that 200 passengers were on board, only four were slightly injured. (*Mr William Jackson*)

have escaped). His site was in the village of Church, on an old cricket field, and the date was 27 January 1942:

Dear Mary,
Once again we're having some rough weather and last night and today has given us a hectic time with the balloon. After being out on various jobs at 10 p.m. and again at 10.45 we turned in, only to be called out again at 4 a.m. in order to 'bed it'. With almost a gale blowing it was a difficult job and eventually some of the hauling-down ropes snapped and made the job impossible, and so now the balloon is careering about, and likely to break away at any moment, but there's nothing more we can do about it unless the cable holds until it calms down. For all that though we did a good job of work in keeping it at all under the circumstances, it was nothing anyone could help and several other sites have lost theirs, not to mention 3 or 4 casualties with broken bones. It's been raining a sort of ice all day. . . .

Chapter Five

A Churchill Tank Called 'Worthy'

It is indeed fortunate that Keighley was not bombed. When the first air-raid warnings sounded in 1940 residents of one short suburban street – in close proximity to a factory target – would gather in the doubtful shelter of a basement wash-house, while a retired hatter, who had served in a Boer War quartermaster's stores without seeing action, patrolled above ground with an air-rifle in case of German paratroopers. (An elderly veteran of the First World War trenches hurried for the wash-house like everybody else.) One old lady stayed in her home, sitting as close as possible to the fire. She had studied photographs of bombed buildings and noticed that quite often their chimney-stacks were left standing, so she thought that was the safest place to be!

Of course, for Keighley even such comedy-dramas formed an exception to the norm. Special Constable Williams, amid his nocturnal observations, could still take note of his natural surroundings, like the December night when 'a flock of ducks passed overhead, one quacking loudly'. His main duty was to caution householders about showing lights, although by September 1940 he felt able to pen a satisfied 'Whitley Head blackout perfect.' He advised residents to stay inside, rather than make 'too much noise out in the road', and he still fussed about the occasional car headlight.

Down in the town itself, Special Constable Alexander Keighley, like Williams a First World War veteran, documented a prosaic routine:

Jan. 27th, 1943. Patrol Duty. 9 p.m. Reported for duty Devonshire St. Kiosk. 9.20. Kings Mill Buffer Depot. 9.40. Russell St. 10 p.m. Point Spencer St. Bottom. 10.40. Hagyard, 3 Rook St. Bedroom window not blacked out. 11 p.m. Point Devonshire St. Kiosk. . . .

Friday, Feb. 12th. Patrol Duty. 9 p.m. Reported at Kiosk Devonshire St. 9.17. Buffer Depot Kings Mill. Went inside O.K. 9.40. Buffer Depot Russell St. 10 p.m. Key Point Spencer St. 11 p.m. Devonshire St. Kiosk. . . .

As this group of local special constables illustrates, men who were no longer young volunteered for service, patrolling in all weathers and taking turns at night duty. Wartime winters tended to be harsh. In the autumn of 1940 Keighley Town Council contributed the opening donation to an appeal for funds to provide winter equipment and 'some measure of comfort' for 'specials' in the Keighley Division. *(George A. Shore/Mrs Annie Wilkinson)*

Saturday, June 26th. Plain Clothes Patrol. 3.15. Guard House estate & allotments. 4.15. Arrived Home. . . .

The buffer depots, incidentally, were emergency food stores.

Over two and a half years Special Constable Keighley's most noteworthy cases seem to have been finding a brown-and-white smooth-haired fox terrier 'sitting in road & unable to walk', checking the name and address on its collar and taking it to the police station; accompanying a woman to a house where a man was 'in drink and causing uproar' (happily he had gone by the time they arrived); and organising the switching off of a light in the staircase window of an empty house.

Nevertheless, Keighley police records show that misdemeanours were widespread at a time when rationing and the necessity for blackouts created a new range of offences. Motor vehicles were checked for unscreened lights, and drivers faced a fine if their bumpers were not painted white. Especially common were householders 'displaying light in a dwelling-house', for which fines could be as high as £2, although a 75-year-old man and a 74-year-old woman were let off with a caution on the grounds of their 'advanced age'. On the other hand, a works superintendent 'permitting light to be displayed' was fined £5.

These regular policemen and Police War Reservists were responsible for law and order in the Worth Valley area. Police Constable Arthur Dykes, seated at the far right, featured in an Oxenhope sensation in 1939 when, having disturbed thieves in the small hours, he and his 17-year-old son were carried some distance on the running-boards of an unlit getaway car while grappling with its occupants. Shots were fired and both were thrown off, but resulting damage to the car enabled the Halifax police to arrest the culprits. *(Mr George Dykes)*

A notable feature of such wartime details is that virtually everybody had an occupation, from a 14-year-old errand-boy to a 68-year-old boilerman. One rare exception, an unemployed young woman, was bound over and ordered to pay fines, costs and damages for breaking a shop window and pointlessly stealing 'two lady's odd shoes'.

A cross-section of the public contrived to fall foul of the law, often owing to wartime circumstances. The culprits' occupations – fitters, turners, grinders, greasers, moulders, scrapers, core makers, comb setters, cap spinners, iron drillers, machine pressers, jobber lads, borers and screwers – reflected the industrial nature of the locality; while summonses, mainly for motoring offences, were also served on a deputy head warden, a police telephone operator, an inspector of naval ordnance, an aircraft inspector and an aircraft engineer, a munitions inspector, an evacuation officer, a Home Guard training officer, a Ministry of Food official, a Ministry of Supply officer, an Auxiliary fireman and a National Fire Service dispatch-rider.

Truly, the law brooked no favourites. Even a Military Police truck and motorcyclist were pulled up for speeding in a built-up area. Occasionally, though, a human approach is evident. The driver of a motor-van who had

The variety of part-time services on the home front is illustrated by this group of employees of Darling and Sellers Ltd, machine tool makers of Airedale Works. They range through Civil Defence, the Home Guard and the Auxiliary Fire Service to the diminutive young Army cadet seated at bottom left. *(Mr Jack Hodgson)*

Members of the Keighley National Savings League in 1941, prior to a presentation of the cups on the table to the winning 'works with a preponderance of male labour' and 'with over 50% of female labour'. Chartered accountant Clifford A. Harrison, seated third from the left, would be awarded both the OBE and the CBE for his work in National Savings. Standing second from the right is Wyndham Rowland, editor of the *Keighley News* from 1906 to 1950. *(Mr F.G. Lougee)*

30 November 1940. Sir Noel Curtis-Bennett, at the microphone, opens Keighley's War Weapons Week in a wintry Town Hall Square . . .

'failed to keep records of hours' in 1941 was sent on his way with a caution because he was taking medical supplies to repeatedly bombed Hull.

Usually, however, the exigencies of war demanded stern measures. A garage proprietor 'supplying petrol without coupons' was fined £5, the motorist 'acquiring petrol without coupons' £10. The garage attendant was cautioned by order of the Chief Constable. Accepting 'illegal transfer of a clothing coupon book' could cost the fashion-conscious £5. An attempted suicide got fourteen days' imprisonment, while two 15-year-olds caught stealing from a gas meter were committed to an Approved School – to which each went along with his gas mask, ration book and identity card.

Offenders accused of more serious crimes had the contents of their pockets and handbags listed in the records. A quarryman arrested in 1942 while 'representing himself to be a police officer' was carrying a silver watch and chain, a pair of metal armbands, three keys, a leather purse, a wallet, a cigarette-case, a tobacco-pouch, two briar pipes, a copper cigarette-lighter and a cigarette-holder, a snuffbox, a pocket knife, a propelling pencil, 2s 6d in cash

. . . and marks an indicator already standing at more than £400,000. *(Keighley News/Keighley Reference Library)*

Alderman Joseph Denby, Mayor of Keighley, rides through town in an armoured carrier during War Weapons Week. *(Keighley Reference Library)*

and his identity card. Deemed unfit to plead, he was escorted to the asylum. A 19-year-old cinema usherette, arrested in 1943 for stealing a gold ring, carried her sweet ration coupons, two clothing books, her identity card, a tie-pin, a comb, some photographs and *2s 6d* in her brown leather handbag.

The property of deserters and servicemen absent without leave was routinely listed while they were remanded in custody to await a military escort. Incidentally, this was a most informative type of police record, circumventing the censorship of the period to inform us that, for example, the 71st Light Anti-Aircraft Regiment was at Askham Bryan and the Pioneer Corps at Valley Parade, Bradford; No. 1 Bomb Disposal Company of the Royal Engineers at Leeds and the 6th Home Defence Battalion of the East Lancashire Regiment at Pendleton.

Detainees almost always carried cigarette-lighters and cases (the cigarettes were counted) and pathetically small amounts of money, together with combs, penknives and fountain pens. One not quite typical deserter had 'cash *2s 5d*, fountain pen, wallet etc., private papers, pawn ticket No. 3798, Army Pay book, gas mask, 2 combs in case, field dressing, razor blades, pencil, gramophone handle, identity disk, bottle opener and hat badge'. The gramophone handle is thought-provoking!

With a regular police force substantially augmented by special constables and the full-time War Reserve, no offence was too small to be pursued. Gaming with cards entailed a 5s fine, horses straying on the highway 10s, indecent language 20s. Dogs without a licence, or without a name on the collar, or roaming at night, or dangerous and out of control could cost their owners anything from 5s to 17s 9d.

Each August and September brought its inevitable crop of 'damage to fruit trees' and 'stealing growing apples', always by boys. Even when the owners refused to press charges, parents were still likely to have to pay costs.

Yet in the main Keighley was a decent community. For most people, most of the time, war meant a hard routine of daily life made harder by problems of shortages, rationing, the blackout, overtime war work, fire-watching and a plethora of voluntary efforts, while worrying – and all too often grieving – over absent loved ones.

The compulsory removal of gates and railings was unusual, in that it struck a deep chord of resentment. Those protecting Keighley's public parks were the first to go, in September 1940, the authorities realising that this left the parks wide open all night but naively believing that 'the good sense of the townsfolk will keep people from staying in the park beyond the recognised hours'.

Later, although in some cases not until 1942, it was the turn of private houses to lose their gates and railings. 'Owners', those complaining were blandly told, 'will have to accept it as a contribution to the war effort'. Jagged stumps left by contractors made matters worse. Some householders were still trying to claim compensation as late as 1948, when their former gates were assessed at a 1939 second-hand value, 'less a percentage in respect of depreciation', while their railings, 'which when severed lose their original character, have no second-hand value except as scrap metal'.

Other forms of recycling were, however, taken up with some enthusiasm. 'On Saturday afternoon last I paid a flying visit to the 9th Keighley (Albert Street) Headquarters,' wrote a reporter describing the efforts of Boy Scouts in 1939, 'and was amazed at the sight that met my eyes – mass upon mass of waste-paper wherever one's gaze fell!' Scoutmasters and Scouts were 'wading through a veritable mountain of paper' and 'doing their best to sort the paper out into the various categories'. Steeton Scouts had brought their quota in by horse and cart.

By 1940 the local authority was organising weekly collections of paper, metals and bones (in hot weather it was considered necessary to collect the bones more frequently), and pig-food bins made their appearance in every street. During that August Keighley collected 41 tons of waste paper, 34 tons of scrap metal, 6 tons of rags, 2 tons of pig food, 1 ton of bones and 79 dozen

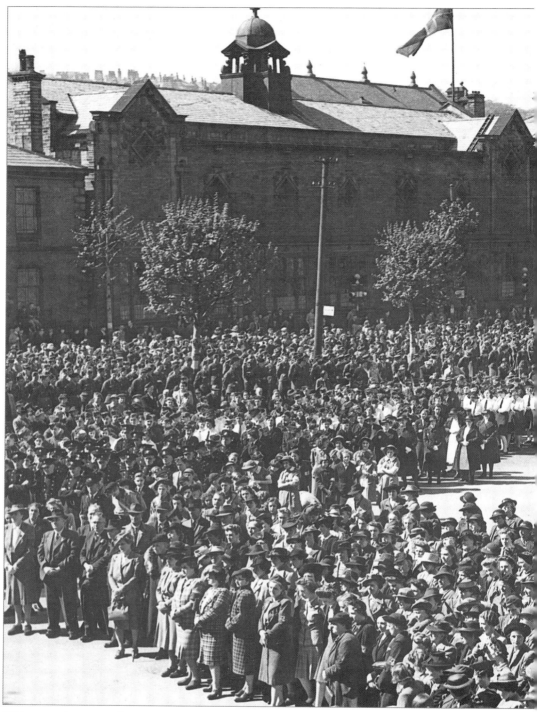

This was the scene in the Town Hall Square on Saturday 15 May 1943, as a parade of services and voluntary organisations listens to an address by Rear Admiral Dennis Boyd,

Fifth Sea Lord and Head of the Fleet Air Arm, at the start of Wings for Victory Week. By the following Saturday Keighley would have raised £1,453,147. *(Author's collection)*

Her Royal Highness the Princess Royal walking along North Street with the Mayor, Mr Tom Snowden, half-way through Keighley's Wings for Victory Week, 1943. *(Author's collection)*

jars. A book salvage drive in 1943 produced nearly 200,000 volumes, the Director of Cleansing rejoicing that the public had 'put patriotism before antiquarian sentiment'. Irrevocably, old-established firms had cleared out their records dating back to the Industrial Revolution, and the Post Office its archives from stagecoach days. The great majority of books were repulped, though reassuringly some were rescued for use by the Forces or children's hospitals, a select few finding their way into libraries.

One especially popular means of helping the war effort was provided by National Savings, which were strenuously promoted, women in particular being encouraged to form street groups, while a Keighley National Savings League aimed 'to foster enthusiasm for savings in works and factories'. The Bradford *Telegraph and Argus* sponsored a trophy for the best savings among 'works with a preponderance of male labour', and the *Keighley News* another for those 'with over

Wings for Victory Week, 1943. The Princess Royal, having ceremonially marked the Town Hall Square indicator at £897,520, stands in the middle of local members of the Red Cross, of which she was Commandant-in-Chief of the British Detachments. *(Author's collection)*

50% of female labour'. At their first presentation in 1941, H. Widdop and Co. Ltd won the *Telegraph and Argus* cup, and Fred Hurtley Ltd the *Keighley News* cup.

More than anything else, however, the great set-piece special fund-raising weeks, interspersed throughout the war, brought out the community's financial

Wings for Victory Week, Silsden, 1943. Hubert Fortune and John Hustwick, members of the Flying Club, and Leading Aircraftwoman Joyce Bancroft, a Silsden girl working with the RAF pigeon service, are about to release one of their 185 fund-raising and message-bearing birds. *(Mrs Webster)*

Dr J.J. Brigg, who had just been made a Freeman of the Borough, opens a Keighley and District Red Cross 'Rally' Week in August 1942, the primary aim of which was to recruit collectors for a Penny-a-Week Fund. He is describing an estimated '100,000 prisoners of war in Germany and under German domination' in receipt of Red Cross parcels, but most of his platform party do not appear to be really listening. The attentive exception, at the right-hand end of the upper row, was Dr William Scatterty, County Commissioner for the St John Ambulance Brigade. *(William Speight)*

best. War Weapons Week, from 30 November to 7 December 1940, set itself a target of £500,000 to pay for 21 bombers and 8,000 bombs – a sum that had been reached by the Monday morning, mainly by the sale of National Savings Certificates, National War and Defence Bonds, investments at the Post Office and York County Trustee Savings Banks, and interest-free loans.

Such weeks were spectacular occasions. Sir Noel Curtis-Bennett, KCVO, launched Keighley's War Weapons Week by setting an indicator in the Town Hall Square and taking the salute at a parade of the military, the Home Guard, the Air Defence Cadet Corps, Women's Voluntary Services, the St John Ambulance Brigade, air-raid wardens and special constables, the Observer Corps and first-aid parties, the Auxiliary Fire Service, Boy Scouts and Girl Guides . . . a growing census of war workers. Such was public interest that his subsequent address was disseminated by radio relay.

A German Messerschmitt, described as 'battle-scarred', went on show in the Town Hall Square, and there were displays of photographs and schoolchildren's

Fund-raising could be a genteel affair. This was the opening of a garden party in aid of the Women's Voluntary Services Comforts Fund, at 'Withens', Oakworth, the home of Mr and Mrs Alfred Newsholme, in August 1940. Attractions included clock golf, a treasure hunt, a troupe of 'dainty dancers' and music by the Haworth Prize Brass Band. *(Keighley News/William Speight)*

posters in the Air Cadet headquarters, plus a suspended parachute. The week raised a total of £1,040,435, representing £18 7s 5d per head of population. Keighley Corporation and the Keighley and Craven Building Society had contributed £50,000 each; Prince-Smith and Stells Ltd and Robert Clough (Keighley) Ltd £30,000 each; and other banks and building societies £25,000 each.

Keighley Warship Week, in March 1942, raised £1,320,126 or £23 8s 4½d per head of population, almost doubling an objective of £700,000 to cover the cost of HMS destroyer *Marne*. Admiral Sir Roger Keyes was to have taken the salute at the initial parade, but as he was ill Rear Admiral the Hon. Lionel Forbes-Sempill came instead. The occasion was marred for three respectable members of the Keighley and District Photographic Association, who found themselves hauled before the magistrates and their films seized for 'taking a photograph of an assembly of His Majesty's Forces, without a permit'.

Some Riddlesden fund-raisers who asked if their £77 3s 9d, acquired with the aid of a sailor doll, could be earmarked towards a ship's compass for HMS *Marne* epitomise the community dimension of such efforts:

The doll's boots were made and presented by Mr White, of Queen Street, Keighley, who is an ex-sailor, the socks were knitted by Mrs Rushworth, of Canal Road, Riddlesden, who has made 86 pairs of socks for men in the Navy, and the lanyard was made by a sailor. The doll was dressed by Mrs McNicoll, of Bar Lane, Riddlesden.

Keighley had hoped to win a National Savings County Championship Flag to fly from its Town Hall, but the system of awarding this on a head-of-population basis favoured smaller communities, where a few larger contributors could substantially boost the average – hence Denby Dale got the flag.

However, one Keighley benefit from Warship Week was its adoption of HMS *Marne*, whose Able Seaman editor of the ship's magazine, *The Buzz*, wrote asking for contributions from townspeople, and suggested featuring an essay competition for Keighley schoolchildren. The winner, a 12-year-old Ingrow boy, was sent 'a handsome box of chocolates'. An officer and five ratings later visited Keighley for a ceremonial exchange of plaques in the Town Hall Square, the Mayor presenting the ship with a Borough coat-of-arms and receiving a *Marne* crest in return.

Wings for Victory Week took place from 15 to 22 May 1943, when Keighley aimed to raise £750,000, the cost of ten Lancasters and seventy-five Spitfires. Highlight in mid-week was a visit from the Princess Royal, who ceremonially marked an indicator already standing at £897,520. She also inspected a guard of honour from the WAAF and the Keighley Girls' Training Corps and called in at the Technical College, the Hospital Supplies Depot and the Woodbine Day Nursery, where forty-seven children of war-working mothers sat in the garden having tea, wearing sun-bonnets made by staff specially for the occasion.

By the end of the week Keighley had raised £1,453,147 or £26 18s 11d per head of population. Organisers had confidently expected to win the County Championship Flag, but Ripponden delayed announcing their figure until half an hour after Keighley's, thus learning what they had to beat and gaining themselves time to top it. Keighley accepted defeat with fairly good grace, while commenting that perhaps there ought to be a second flag to be awarded to larger towns.

A follow-up 'Bomb Up the Bombers' campaign the following year raised £214,225, financing enough bombs for 'almost' eighteen raids by the Lancasters provided by Wings for Victory Week – this was 'eight raids above the target of ten raids'.

Meanwhile Silsden's Wings for Victory Week, though featuring such standard activities as a football match between Cadets and an Army team (the Army won) and a play (*Love in a Mist* performed by the Ilkley Players), added a novel detail. The wartime use of messenger pigeons had created a revival of interest in a Silsden and District Flying Club (albeit its members were

A shift from the bayonet department at the Burlington Shed of Prince-Smith and Stells Ltd poses in Dalton Lane. During the war they produced a total of 1,057,515 spike bayonets. *(George A. Shore/Mrs Irene Robertshaw)*

This homely snapshot of office staff on the eve of a wartime Christmas is unusual in that it was taken in the Steeton Royal Ordnance Factory where, for security reasons, photographs were forbidden! The simplicity of the decorations suggests the bleakness of the period. *(Mr Michael Shearing)*

required, under defence regulations, to hold permits to keep homing pigeons). Now some purchasers of Savings Certificates were allowed to send greetings to local friends by 'pigeon post'. Some 185 birds, 'bearing messages on their legs secured by a small rubber ring', were dispatched from the Playing Fields; then when they returned to their lofts, the messages were delivered by hand. If from a purely practical point of view this seems a slightly pointless exercise, it aroused a good deal of interest and helped towards Silsden's total of £160,664.

In April 1944 it was the turn of Salute the Soldier Week, with a Keighley target of £750,000, the cost of equipping a battalion from each of Yorkshire's six infantry regiments. The Earl of Harewood, Lord Lieutenant of the County, took the salute at a parade mustering no fewer than five bands – those of the Duke of Wellington's Regiment, Bradford Sea Scouts, the Keighley Squadron of the Air Training Corps, Haworth Public Prize Band and the Canal Ironworks Silver Band – before addressing the crowds and marking an indicator already up to nearly £379,000.

Early in the week an open-air service was held on the football field. Famous actor Bransby Williams appeared in a concert at the Ritz Cinema, and Captain Derek McCullock ('Uncle Mac' of the BBC's *Children's Hour*) spoke in the Town Hall Square and the Municipal Hall. By the end of Salute the Soldier Week Keighley had raised £1,102,941 or £20 15s 4d per head of population. This was less than the two previous fund-raising Weeks, but as larger investors tended to diminish smaller ones were saving more, and at last Keighley was able to fly the County Championship Flag.

Fund-raising was by no means confined to the special Weeks. A longer-running 'Tanks for Attack' campaign in 1942 netted £235,858. The Keighley Savings Committee was invited to name the resulting Churchill tank, driven, appropriately, by a Yorkshireman from Leeds. Its members suggested 'Worthy', adapted from the Borough coat-of-arms motto 'By Worth', which was duly painted on the turret. The Committee also sent cigarettes for the driver to distribute among the crew.

Another appeal, aimed at providing a Keighley merchant ship, closed at £271,951, which represented a vessel of 10,878 tons. Hopes of this being christened SS *Keighley* were dashed on account of there having been 'a certain amount of leakage of information in towns where ships had been specifically named'. Keighley had to be content with the gift of a symbolic 'Red Duster' flag of the Merchant Service.

In 1943, encouraged by a local Anglo-Soviet Committee, Keighley became one of the first towns attempting to 'adopt' a community in the Soviet Union. Yaroslavl, a city on the Volga, was chosen mainly because its textile and engineering industries were similar to Keighley's. A mass meeting in the Ritz cinema drafted a cable: 'The people of Keighley send to the people of Yaroslavl

Queen Elizabeth during her visit to the Royal Ordnance Factory at Steeton in 1942. Photographers were not allowed inside the buildings. *(Margery Moore)*

greetings on this Red Army anniversary day, with best wishes for the continued successes of the Red Army in the common cause.' Alas, two years later no reply had been forthcoming!

An Anglo-Soviet Public Relations Appeal proved more positive in 1944, when Keighley contributed £1,000 towards a Stalingrad Hospital Fund, providing seven beds. A Borough coat-of-arms, to be displayed in the hospital, was duly forwarded with a message 'To the Citizens of Stalingrad from the Citizens of Keighley' acknowledging 'the historic defence of the City by

the Citizens of Stalingrad through whose fortitude and unshakeable courage the power of Nazism was broken'.

Closer to home, an annual egg collection accumulated 8,606 in 1941 for patients in the Keighley and District Victoria Hospital. The following year, when eggs had become rationed, the main appeal was to poultry-keepers with fifty or fewer hens who were still 'free to give eggs away' – these could be handed in at designated grocers' and butchers' or at places of worship, or at a hut for the purpose in the Town Hall Square. By 1943 the poultry-keepers capable of giving eggs away were down to those with fewer than twenty-five hens. In 1945 the slogan was 'One egg is not too small a gift'.

Of course, support for so many causes could not always rise to superhuman levels. A meeting organised by a Keighley Aid to Greece Committee in 1942 drew an extremely disappointing audience, and Keighley's Red Cross Penny-a-Week Fund lagged behind those of many other West Riding towns. A Red Cross 'Rally' Week aimed to recruit more collectors 'to go from door to door in a systematic manner' collecting weekly pennies with which to send parcels to prisoners of war. The 15,000 households in the Borough might ideally have raised upwards of £60 a week, but understandably this was not achieved.

A Haworth branch of the Red Cross, formed in 1942, raised £834 8s 11½d during its first year, largely by means of a gift shop, a whist drive and dance, and a summer fair (although it was realistically minuted 'that any further sports connected with the Country Fair be abandoned owing to the inclement weather'). A Red Cross trailer film was shown at the Brontë Cinema, followed by a retiring collection taken by committee members and girls from the Guides and the Training Corps. Thirty-five collectors averaged between them £17 a month, while customers failing to bring their own bags to bakers' shops were expected to put something in a Red Cross box. A flag day in 1944 realised

This group from the milling department at Prince-Smith and Stells Ltd illustrates women's workwear, each with a 'PSK' tag on the left breast. For once we know all their names. Top row, left to right: Stella Walls, Madge Horsley, Jim Hall, Florence Huggitt, Amy Cavanagh. Bottom row: Harriet Goodby, May Kenny, Helena Stephenson, Alice Bates. *(Mrs Mary S. McLelland)*

£13 6s, another whist drive and dance only £8 5s. In two and a half years the Haworth Red Cross branch totalled £1,811 12s 10d.

But most vital of all in the local war effort was industrial production. The records of wartime businesses reveal some bizarre twists of fate. The London branch of a German firm of leather goods manufacturers relocated to Keighley, where there was less risk of bombing, moving into the mostly unoccupied Airedale Mills and switching to the production of Army webbing, subsequently becoming known as Keighley Bagcraft Ltd and equipping, among others, French Resistance fighters and the first 50,000 American troops in Britain. Their manager, Peter Black, born in Berlin in 1908, was to loom large indeed in postwar industrial Keighley.

The British NSF Co. Ltd had been German when founded in 1932. Bombed out of Croydon in 1940, the firm came to Keighley as the British National Switch Factory, occupying Dalton Mills and making electrical components that included parts for the radios used by the Resistance in occupied Europe, together with 'many hush-hush appliances that were put to vital national use in radar, communications, and aircraft equipment'.

At the very end of July 1939 the directors of machine-tool manufacturers Prince-Smith and Stells Ltd had appointed a German agent to represent them in Bohemia, Moravia and the controversial Sudetenland. Thereafter, however, directors' meetings followed a patriotic pattern of support for good causes – a £25,000 interest-free loan for War Weapons Week, another £25,000 in War Bonds for Wings for Victory Week, a £250 contribution to the Bradford District Red Cross Appeal in 1944 – and Government contracts. The latter ranged from 'Case Strikers for QF 25 pdr. MK II Breach Mechanism' and '3-inch Tank Howitzer Breach Mechanisms' to '25 pdr. Chemical Shell Containers', '2 pdr. A.P. Shot' and 'Fuse 117'. The firm undertook 'machining of 40 M/M A.A. H.E. Shells' and 'machining of Bayonets No. 4 Mark IIA at the rate of 9500 per week (forgings to be supplied)'. Repeatedly the Ministry of Supply paid for additional plant and equipment. In 1944 the Ministry of Aircraft Production agreed to 'expand the Company's Capacity in connection with the conversion of American Aircraft'.

In the course of the war Prince-Smith and Stells Ltd produced – among much else – 661,910 Bren-gun magazine platforms, 333,654 Wellington aircraft parts, 107,154 hand grenades and 1,057,515 spike bayonets. Their workforce rose from a pre-war 1,700 to 3,500, some 1,300 of whom were women. One of them recalls how two weeks on day-shift alternated with two on nights. An unpleasant liquid running constantly over their machines caused dermatitis on their hands.

Meanwhile at Steeton the Royal Ordnance Factory, popularly known as 'The Dump', started production early in 1941 and by August 1945 had turned out 204 million munition components, including 63 million shells and 120 million 20mm cases. At its peak it employed over 4,000, two-thirds of whom were women, many drafted there as an alternative to conscription into the Forces. Workers were brought by special trains and buses from sixty-two towns and villages in Yorkshire and Lancashire, as far apart as Bradford, Nelson and Barnoldswick; there were also many girls from Ireland. Staff provided most of their own lunch-time entertainment but qualified for an ENSA concert once a fortnight. 'The Dump' even ran a 7-acre farm, keeping up to thirty pigs at a time and supplying its canteen with pork and vegetables. Two shop stewards, Mrs W. Feeney and Mrs M. Stovold, were awarded the MBE.

The Howden Hall hostel, near Silsden, with its eight blocks named after Yorkshire rivers, was built by the Ministry of Supply in 1942 originally to house a big draft of Royal Ordnance Factory workers, although during the next three years it was to accommodate, for varying periods, a motley population of 3,000 war workers, Land Army girls, bombed-out Londoners, welfare officers and office staff. The hostel also merited ENSA entertainments and hosted the Ballet Rambert's first engagement on behalf of the Council for the Encouragement of Music and the Arts.

In March 1942 King George VI and Queen Elizabeth visited what the press could only guardedly call 'a North-Eastern factory' – in reality 'The Dump'. Despite media secrecy and an absence of public announcements, news of their coming was well-known locally, so that when they passed through Keighley itself their route was lined with cheering schoolchildren. Some firms let their employees out for the occasion, this being the first visit to Keighley of a reigning monarch since 1918, when George V and Queen Mary had similarly helped boost wartime morale.

Queen Elizabeth toured the factory's two surgeries and spoke to workers, being told how 'every soldier's wife had holiday when her husband came home on leave'. The Queen admired the 1,000-seater canteen with its stage for entertainments.

'They tell me', she reportedly observed to Miss Kathleen Gardner, assistant canteen manageress, 'that your stage was made out of packing cases'.

'Yes, your Majesty,' came the reply. 'Packing cases that brought machines from America.'

'I think that's awfully good work,' responded the Queen. 'It's a nice canteen. I like the homely atmosphere.'

Another important concern was H. Widdop and Co. Ltd, whose marine engines in 1939 were 'just what the Admiralty and Ministry of Shipping required'. The exploits of Widdop engines on the eve of war read like a tale by Kipling. Many were meant for coastal craft and inland waterways barges, but they also powered vessels that had made non-stop runs to Freetown in Sierra Leone and Lagos in Nigeria. There were Widdop engines in Sarawak and Papua, in a ferry at Calabar in West Africa and a dredger in the harbour at Goa in Portuguese India. Widdop diesel engines ran the launches supplying Imperial Airways Empire seaplanes, while the 'stone for increasing the height of the Assiut Dam on the River Nile was being towed to the site of the work by a 240bhp tug re-engined with Keighley machinery'.

In 1938 Widdop's had been completing eight large engines for Chinese river boats. In the event most of these escaped capture by the Japanese 'by making a long voyage to India non-stop'. Inevitably the war brought expansion to Widdop's. 'One officer told the marine engine builders in Keighley', the firm later advertised with an example, 'that one of their units had been instrumental in saving hundreds of wounded Australians from capture. The machinery operated continuously day and night, and rescue and patrol work never ceased until the boat was badly damaged.'

Staff of the Woodbine Day Nursery take their young charges – children of mothers on war work – for a walk or a ride along Skipton Road, about 1943. The white bands painted round the tree on the right made it more visible in the blackout. *(Mrs Kate Nicholls)*

The traditional diversity of Keighley industries was further reflected in Wimsol Ltd of Atlas Mills, which made soaps, cleansing agents, anti-dermatitis creams and disinfectants 'for firms engaged on essential work in the national interest'; and George Hattersley and Sons Ltd of Greengate Shed, who, by 1945, had made 'enough webbing to encircle the world, and then some – a length of 50 million yards or over 28,000 miles' for the Ministry of Supply! One of their specialities was the narrow fabrics used in balloons, parachutes and dinghies. It was appropriate that in 1943 their workers listened to an address by a flying-officer who had actually used both a parachute and a dinghy.

Hattersley's 800-strong workforce additionally produced a versatile engineering range: steering and balance gear a ssemblies for 2-pounder and 6-pounder guns, Bofors guns and howitzers; parts for tanks, armoured vehicles and Bailey bridges; mine-sweeping devices and special looms for weaving airmen's clothing. By 1945 they had made 8,000 projector infantry anti-tank guns.

Dean, Smith and Grace Ltd were able from the beginning to produce complete lathes to government requirements without having to subcontract. From their pre-war average of forty lathes a month the output at their 1942 peak was a hundred a month, mainly for the three Services, the Ministry of Supply, the Admiralty – for use aboard repair ships – and Russia. Dean, Smith and Grace was the first Keighley all-male firm to employ women, at most a hundred, who were 'quick to learn the job and adapt themselves to the exacting work'.

By March 1941 – ahead of women's conscription – Keighley's first female machine operators had been taking an eight-week course at the Technical College. They included former weavers, domestic servants and shop assistants, plus a café manageress, a shorthand typist and a probationer nurse, now training to take men's places in engineering firms. 'The trainees certainly add splashes of colour to an otherwise drab workshop,' commented a reporter, watching some on lathes and others shaping and drilling.

Once female conscription was in force, job advertisements for women in engineering were, however urgent, careful to exclude 'those between the ages of 18 and 31' who may be required for other, compulsory duties; younger and older applicants were promised 'clean assembly work or light machine operations under ideal working conditions; standard rates of pay, plus bonus'. An exhibition at the Electricity Showrooms (a popular display venue) emphasised 'the types of work at present being done by Women War Workers'. By 1944 even the signals and points on the Worth Valley branch line were being operated by women.

The land presented a special problem at harvest-time. In 1943 the customary itinerant Irish haymakers were asking from £24 to £34 for a month's work, plus board and lodgings – more than double their pre-war rate. Appeals were accordingly made 'to all those who could to give some of their spare time' to help. School pupils, whose summer camps at Humphrey Head and Kirkcudbright had been closed for the duration, were encouraged to go harvesting instead.

A local employer of the Women's Land Army was Fred Sharp's Hatcheries at Oakworth, which provided an often bracing experience in the Worth Valley weather. 'Girls packing day-olds in the hatchery and four-week-olds in the brooder houses were able to keep both dry and warm,' recalls Nesta Hoyle, who worked on an outdoor packing team, 'but at times envied our weather-beaten or sun-tanned complexion'. Her tasks included visiting farms over a 40-mile radius to collect hatching eggs, testing breeding stock for bacillary white diarrhoea and dispatching cartons of chickens from Oakworth Station. Sexing of day-old chicks was originally done by trained Japanese, 'but shortly before Pearl Harbour, they disappeared like snow in summer'.

Women going out to work faced in many cases a difficulty that a Maternity and Child Welfare Committee addressed in 1942 by introducing a child-minding scheme: 'In order to liberate women for essential war work, an Appeal is made to other women to consider the possibility of looking after workers' children during working periods.' The scheme paid an 'acknowledgement' of a shilling per child per day. On an organised basis, the Woodbine Day Nursery in Skipton Road, costing 5s a week, opened late in 1941 with accommodation for thirty children – this later increased – complete with beds and two baths. More day nurseries for under-fives followed, at Victoria Park, Eastwood, Worth Village, Strong Close and Haworth.

For paper-tube manufacturers John Stell and Sons Ltd – who had always employed women – war production necessitated expansion from their Holme and Victoria Mills into extra premises in Kensington Street, where an assembly-line strapped together three tubes to make carrying-cases for 3in mortar bombs. Other speciality tubes were for wrapping parachute cords. An inspector from the Ministry of Defence checked quality.

The natural hazard of working with inflammable materials was vividly demonstrated on 11 January 1945, when the main buildings at Stell's Holme Mills were gutted in what was considered 'the most spectacular blaze in the district for many years' – a disaster immediately immortalised in local folklore, with snow a mile away in the town pink from the glow. The National Fire Service issued a general call, appliances converging from Keighley, Silsden, Ilkley, Bingley and Bradford; two firemen were injured. Production was of course disrupted, but significantly in the case of government contracts, arrangements were immediately made 'through the Federation of Paper Tube Manufacturers to ensure that customers' supplies were maintained as far as possible'.

A carefully posed group in the works canteen at the Messrs W. Slingsby and Co. Ltd foundry in 1943 – boilerman John Edward Tatham is being presented simultaneously with War Savings certificates by Walter Slingsby on the right, and with a cheque on behalf of the employees by Walter Broadfoot on the left. Mary Saxton, the 19-year-old girl he had rescued from the mill dam, and the Chairman of the Keighley Amateur Swimming Club, look on. *(Keighley News/Mrs M. Carter)*

The Holme Mills fire left numerous problems: a big, old-fashioned safe, with all the wages inside, had seized up with the heat, and wet banknotes had to be dried out on the Victoria Mills steam pipes before anybody could be paid; women thrown out of work had to present themselves at the Labour Exchange, in dread of being drafted into bus-conducting; and all the Holme Mills cats (a necessity on the North Beck site where rats were rife) perished in the blaze.

Work could indeed hold unexpected dangers. One December midnight in 1942 two girls on a night-shift at the foundry of Messrs W. Slingsby and Co. Ltd set off across the mill-yard to the canteen. In the blackout they took a wrong turn and walked into a mill dam 9ft deep. One girl struggled out and raised the alarm, whereupon boilerman John Edward Tatham jumped in fully clothed and rescued the other. He was subsequently awarded a Royal Humane Society Testimonial and a Yorkshire Amateur Swimming Club Certificate of Valour for his 'resource and courage on a cold night'.

Chapter Six

'A Tendency to Damp one's Ardour'

Despite the war, of course, some aspects of normal life continued. In 1940, for example, Keighley opened its art deco bus station offices, housing a waiting-room and such staff facilities as a room where conductors could 'make up their tickets and cash in' – a basic but substantial improvement. By 1944 much time and effort were being put into planning an ambitious new town centre divided into five zones. These were to represent sites for civic and government administration; business and professional premises; shops; warehousing and light industry; and recreation and entertainment, complete with an inner ring road. The scheme would have entailed a dramatic redistribution of the existing library, post office, cinemas, theatre, bus station, market and Town Hall (a new Town Hall was envisaged in Bridge Street). In a Council Chamber hung with maps that emphasised 'the magnitude of the scheme', the pipe dream was understandably and indefinitely postponed. Its only feature eventually to materialise decades later was a bypass from Bradford Road to Halifax Road.

Politics could not be so readily deferred. Late in 1941 the Labour Member of Parliament for the Keighley Division died suddenly. Hastings Bertrand Lees-Smith, aged 63 and an asthma sufferer, had been in and out of Parliament on Keighley's behalf (much more in than out) since 1922. He had led a distinguished career, serving as Postmaster-General and President of the Board of Education, and latterly as Leader of the Opposition and acting chairman of the Parliamentary Labour Party. His eventual memorial plaque would be unveiled by no less than Deputy Prime Minister Clement R. Attlee.

Discussion of any consequent by-election was described at the time as 'the most carefree in the history of the Division'. The Keighley Labour Party's choice of a successor fell on Ivor Thomas, of Hereford. Aged 36, holder of an Oxford Double First and a Blue for athletics and cross-country running, biographer, broadcaster and serving Army officer with a potentially roving commission, he had been a sub-editor on *The Times* and chief leader-writer for the *News Chronicle*. To crown all this, he had married Miss Joan Bulmer of the well-known cider family.

Keighley's other parties declined, in gentlemanly fashion, to put candidates forward, and a Bradford Independent who briefly threatened a contest withdrew. Ivor Thomas was returned unopposed, duly expressing his 'debt of gratitude to the Conservative and Liberal parties'.

The following winter he put Keighley on the parliamentary map when his motion for the Sunday opening of theatres and music-halls caused a national sensation. He was shouted down in the House; the Archbishop of Canterbury voiced his disapproval; and the Lord's Day Observance Society offered up public prayers for the good of his soul ('May God deal with Ivor Thomas as He dealt with Saul of Tarsus!') and the defeat of his 'God-dishonouring proposals'. Mr Thomas urbanely suggested that his critics should 'read Mark 2, verses 27 and 28, Luke 13, verses 14 and 15, and John 5, verse 18' ('And he said unto them, The sabbath was made for man, and not man for the sabbath: Therefore the Son of Man is Lord also of the sabbath', etc.).

Repercussions expanded controversially into the theatrical world itself, with Robert Donat (*The Younger Mr Pitt*) publicly declaring, 'You cannot replace the actors' Sunday by a week day', while a sparkling line-up which included Noël Coward, Ivor Novello, John Gielgud, Emlyn Williams and Vivien Leigh formed a Campaign of Actors for Sunday Theatres. Meanwhile Keighley, whose Town Council disapproved of Sunday bowls as 'part of a larger campaign for making Sunday like any other day' and where the Free Church Council had been 'keeping watch on' the odd Sunday cricket match since the previous summer, viewed their MP's proposals with very mixed feelings indeed.

The physical townscape was changing, the parks, already accommodating public air-raid shelters, especially taking the strain. The National Fire Service erected temporary huts there for an 'annual acknowledgement' of a shilling a hut. More prefabricated structures housed day nurseries. Static water supply tanks restricted seating space in the Town Hall Square, and the Imperial War Graves Commission reserved Section R at Utley Cemetery 'for the burial of members of H.M. Forces'. The Ministry of War Transport peremptorily proposed to commandeer the Corporation's diesel road rollers for national service, 'either by agreement or by requisition'. Even the attendant of the Ladies' Convenience in High Street was 'required to undertake work of national importance' instead! Trees at Steeton were controversially felled to support 'the country's need for timber', though the 1st Haworth Guide Company, inspired by an appeal in their *Guide* magazine, raised the wherewithal for a hundred sycamores, which the Corporation planted, early in 1943, on the banks of the Sladen Valley Reservoir. 'It is a happy gesture to plant trees,' observed a speaker equally happily at the requisite ceremony, 'for they are the symbol of young life'.

Planting the 1st Haworth Guide Company's hundred sycamores beside the Sladen Valley Reservoir in March 1943. Enterprising photographer William Speight, with a view to selling as many prints as possible, has gathered everybody into this panoramic group. *(William Speight/Mr Keith Sunderland)*

Enclosed with their 1941 rate demands householders found a 'guide to the arrangements and plans for meeting all the emergencies that can arise from an air-raid' and a form on which they were invited to signify what accommodation they could offer in an emergency. Weeks later only 400 forms had been returned out of 16,000 sent out.

Health was an important issue. Year after year, annual reports by the Borough Medical Officer of Health inveighed against overcrowding: 'evacuees, refugees, wartime marriages and combinations of related families finding temporary accommodation have complexed the whole situation'; this had reached a 'chaotic state'. Atmospheric pollution was exacerbated, too: up until 1944 the Ministry of Home Security requested the production of black smoke 'with a view to national defence against air raids'. By 1943 Keighley's Medical Officer was also expressing concern about the incidence of venereal disease and scabies, 'a condition associated with the movement of infected persons in war-time'. The authorities gradually succeeded in minimising infectious diseases, except measles (910 notified cases in 1945) and scabies. 'The public', it was stressed, 'must understand the highly contagious nature of "itch" and the necessity for early diagnosis and treatment'.

For the public, normal life was further complicated by always being supposed to carry a gas-mask and an identity card which had to be produced 'on demand by a Police Officer in uniform or member of H.M. Armed Forces in uniform on duty'; by having to wind up or down a blackout blind morning and night (employees at John Stell and Sons used to make their own in black and green, complete with a tube to roll them up in); and by rationing, with its necessary regulations: 'When shopping, you must not cut out the coupons yourself, but must hand this book to the shopkeeper and let him cut them out. IT IS ILLEGAL FOR THE SHOPKEEPER TO ACCEPT LOOSE COUPONS.'

Starting in January 1940 with bacon and butter at 4oz per person per week, rationing had spread in March to cover meat – by price rather than weight – and then by July to tea, jam, cheese and cooking fats. One egg was allowed per person per fortnight, while a points system allowed the shopper to choose between biscuits or cereals, fruit or fish. By mid-1941 the clothing ration would provide one new outfit a year. One of the many projects of the WVS was a Children's Shoe Exchange, set up in 1943 'to receive outgrown shoes in good condition which parents wish to exchange for larger sizes in similar condition'. Naturally, no coupons were involved.

Extra nourishment was available through communal feeding, in the works canteen or the British Restaurant. Keighley's first 200-seater British Restaurant opened at the beginning of 1942 in the Marlborough Street Congregational Mission. During its first week it served 264 main meals – prepared more than a mile away at Utley Congregational Sunday School – in a single day, prompting the impracticable suggestion that factories might consider staggering their dinner hours. The British Restaurant, like the works canteen, was a great social leveller, as Alderman Duerden implied in his address at the original opening, commenting that, in ensuring 'that every individual got a fair share of the food which was available', his committee was practising 'democratic principles, the principles of equality, fraternity and justice'. More British Restaurants followed a few months later, at Spencer Street and Wesley Place Sunday Schools, including cash-and-carry departments for local residents who had to bring their own crockery or containers. Another at Heber Street in 1943 opened with a comprehensive menu of vegetable soup, roast beef, roast and boiled potatoes, and jam sponge pudding with custard. By then Marlborough Street was averaging 200 meals a day, Spencer Street 270 and Wesley Place 85.

Inevitably, rationing and shortages affected social life. Thus young girls were instructed to bring their own food and cups to the outdoor Brownie Revels, while refreshments at Keighley and Craven Holiday Fellowship dances had to be limited to 'one potted meat sandwich and a bun per person'. Such functions, incidentally, helped raise donations towards the Merchant Services, the Red Cross, Mrs Churchill's Aid to Russia and a host of other funds. In 1940 soldiers stationed locally were allowed in at half-price; by 1941 they were being admitted free.

The minutes describing preparations for a Holiday Fellowship flannel dance at the Britannia Hall in 1940 evoke a typical blacked-out evening's socialising:

Mrs Fowler, Miss M. Parker and Mr W. Jackson each promised to bring a supply of tea for the dance. . . . It was agreed to ask the Clifton Café to supply the buns which the Committee decided should be obtained for the supper. . . . It was decided to ask the caretaker to act as A.R.P. man. . . . It was proposed that an Ambulance Box should be purchased to be used at the Dances in a case of emergency or Air Raid.

By the beginning of 1941 the danger of incendiary bombs necessitated more energy-draining precautions. 'Every factory, every shop, every house, occupied or unoccupied, must have its fire watcher,' decreed the Minister of Home Security. 'You cannot stop a high-explosive bomb from bursting, but you can stop a fire-bomb from starting a fire.' The call of the moment became 'Fall in, the fire-bomb fighters!'

In addition to its fire-fighting service Keighley already had over a thousand volunteers, many of them women, trained in the use of stirrup-pumps, but now much more needed doing. A comprehensive fire-watching scheme emerged, works and businesses drawing up their employees' rotas of duty. The Town Hall thoughtfully provided three camp beds 'with sufficient bedding' for its staff fire-watching parties, together with 'three patent scoops for dealing with incendiary bombs'. Householders formed into fire-watching groups. Sand – a necessity for combating incendiaries – was issued in hundredweight bags to 4,000 premises and distributed about the borough in 240 special bins. The organisation in 1942 of an official, compulsory Fire Guard proved difficult, however. In Keighley, 95 per cent of those thought eligible for fire-watching tried initially to claim exemption, many on the reasonable grounds of being already involved in Civil Defence, though 'one man explained that he had rheumatism and could not get up until his wife had rubbed his back'!

At the same time the Citizens' Advice Bureau had to extend its scope to tackle the potentially myriad problems that would arise in the event of local air-raids. It was placed on a more professional footing by amalgamation with an Information Centre provided by the Ministry of Health, and transferred into the Public Library. Its first planned location in 'the book-binding room' proving inappropriate, it operated instead behind a screen in a corner of the Reference Library.

A bleak atmosphere extended to wider events. Restrictions on leisure travel encouraged the idea of 'stay-at-home' holidays, though in Keighley this was slow to get into its stride. Easter 1942 was 'the first public holiday during the present war that facilities for seeking recreation in other environments were so limited', the *Keighley News* rather ponderously characterised what turned out to be 'about the most sombre holiday on record'. There were no excursion trains, and the buses operated a reduced Sunday service, to the surprise of many who had not anticipated their later starts and earlier return journeys. Even Keighleyites venturing to Bradford were warned they might not get buses back, and some were faced with walking home from as far afield as Colne. For the many staying in Keighley, there was simply the Hippodrome theatre, the cinemas, an Easter Saturday football match and 'a dance or two'. Patronage of all was 'overwhelming', with many unable to get in.

Things were much improved, however, by Keighley Parish Feast that July. The parks were busy with donkey rides, Punch and Judy shows, a funfair, concert parties and the National Fire Service athletic sports. There was an ARP demonstration in Victoria Park, sheepdog trials in the Highfield Recreation Ground, a swimming gala, bands and cricket matches, and a push-ball competition sponsored by the *Daily Mail*.

Intellectual highlight was a 'Brains Trust', whose panel comprised a professor of mathematics, a missionary, a Labour Party organiser, a bookmaker, an Indian barrister, a member of the Russia Today Society, and Ivor Thomas, MP; the questionmaster was William Healey, Technical College Principal and father of a future Chancellor of the Exchequer.

The annual Friendly Societies' Hospital Gala was also able to adapt reasonably well to changed circumstances. By 1943 petrol-driven vehicles were virtually absent from its procession, the sight of town councillors and aldermen riding round in a coach instead of individual motor cars raising 'no little amusement' among the bystanders. On the other hand, the horse had 'come into its own' again, both in competitive classes and drawing the tableaux. Skits on such topical irritations as coupons and rationing added zest to the fancy-dress characters, while the procession offered a marching opportunity for Scouts, Cadets and the Home Guard Band.

Keighley Police No. 1 and No. 2 tug-of-war teams in action in Victoria Park during 'Stay-at-Home' holiday sports in July 1942. No. 1 team (Police Constables Hayhurst, White, Lodge, Cocliff, Coope and Dykes, with Sergeant Tattersall as coach) beat No. 2 (Police Constables Plant and Brooks and Police Reservists Broster, Whittel, Jackson and Arrowsmith, coached by Inspector Driver). *(Mr George Dykes)*

Off-duty nurses enjoying themselves at a garden party in 1944 in aid of the Keighley and District Victoria Hospital. They appear to be poking fun at a baby product called Glaxo, and displaying photographs of themselves as babies, presumably for a competition. *(George A. Shore/Mr Graham Hall)*

Wartime Christmases too were celebrated as cheerfully as possible in the Keighley and District Victoria Hospital, where the nurses traditionally sang carols and put on pantomimes, patients received presents from the Matron's Christmas Fund and a Workpeople's Collection Committee, and Dr Joseph Chalmers, a surgeon there for a quarter of a century, played Santa Claus for the children.

Nevertheless, daily life was beset with inconveniences. 'In consequence of the shortage of labour,' warned the Town Clerk late in 1941, 'it will not be possible this coming winter to give the usual attention to the Clearance of Snow from adopted roads in the Borough'. Since priority would have to be given to keeping the carriageways clear, it 'would help tremendously and be a real contribution to the common good' if each rate-payer would 'clear of snow the footway in front of the property he occupies'. The local Bakers' Association had to request shoppers to reuse their bags and wrapping paper, as there was a shortage. Compulsory queuing for buses was introduced in 1942. Keighley–West Yorkshire Services became concerned about their buses crossing what they regarded as the undermaintained bridges over the Leeds and

The children's Christmas party at Keighley and District Victoria Hospital on Boxing Day 1943. Santa Claus was Dr Joseph Chalmers for many years. *(Mrs Shirley Cannon)*

Liverpool Canal, decreeing that passengers on the Riddlesden and Morton routes respectively should get out and walk over the Granby Lane and Morton Lane bridges. Most seem to have treated this precaution 'jocularly', although indulging in 'satirical comments', for they could see heavily laden lorries crossing without mishap. A special problem regarding mothers with babies attending a Morton Infant Welfare Clinic was resolved 'amicably' by at least one conductor, who allowed them to leave their offspring aboard while they walked across, he himself holding 'a child of six weeks in his arms being carefully nursed'!

Some organisations could be very seriously affected by wartime conditions, as the attenuated minutes of the Keighley Vocal Union attest. 'The outbreak of war upset all other arrangements,' their Annual General Meeting was reminded in 1940. 'To begin with the Belle Vue Competition fixed for Sept. 9 was cancelled and all other Competitions which normally we should have taken part in suffered the same fate.' The blackout, coupled with a severe winter, had virtually scuppered rehearsals. 'It is not possible to see what lies ahead of us,' their secretary understandably lamented in late May 1940. The following year was no better ('the choir to be called together if and when thought desirable'); neither was 1942, when a proposed concert failed to materialise: 'We are

Nursing staff in the Keighley and District Victoria Hospital follow a Christmas tradition by singing carols. *(Mr Graham Hall)*

however unfortunately placed in the matter of meeting under blackout conditions, many of us being out of the Keighley area and dependent on the curtailed 'bus services at present operating.' 'These circumstances', the minutes feelingly observed, 'have a tendency to damp one's ardour'. However, in the latter half of the war the Vocal Union fared rather better, managing to take part in the Brighouse Festival, where they produced some very good singing 'considering our handicaps as to numbers and balance of parts'. In 1944 they presented *Hiawatha* in aid of the Red Cross Fund.

But for the Keighley Motor Club, hard hit by petrol rationing, there seemed no alternative in 1940 to winding itself up and distributing its funds to local charities and causes. The Fire Brigade Friendly Society discontinued its traditional collection of Christmas tips and by order of the Chief Officer disbanded its Incidental Fund. A retrospective note in the Knowle Park Congregational Chapel minute-book charts the decline of a typical cricket club:

It was decided to withdraw the second team from the League in June 1940 owing to shortage of players. The first team carried on until the end of the season. During the winter efforts were made to keep the club going, but this was found impossible, the club, therefore, suspended activities.

Members of the Keighley Temperance Society, with their hall requisitioned by the military, were compelled to curtail their normal activities, although they discussed 'the question of work amongst the soldiers in the Recreation Room' and were rewarded in 1940 with a letter from the Commanding Officer of the 2/6th Duke of Wellington's Regiment 'expressing thanks on behalf of all ranks for all the work done for the happiness, comfort and morale of the troops'. They were also able to find a purpose in voicing their concerns about 'the continued supply of barley and sugar to the breweries when animal foodstuffs are insufficient and sugar is severely rationed'. They sent a deputation to that effect to MP Mr Lees-Smith.

Their female counterparts, the Little White Ribboners (who seem rather to have espoused total abstinence), also discussed 'entertaining the soldiers' and sent similar resolutions to the Food Controller and the Prime Minister as well as Mr Lees-Smith. Their *White Ribbon Magazine* was dispatched 'to His Majesty's Ship the *Renown* to get our soldiers, sailors and airmen interested in our work'. Possibly more usefully, £1 went 'to the blinded children of Warrington, who were blinded at a garden party for the Spitfire Fund by being bombed'.

The supply of sugar and cereals to brewers greatly exercised the discussions of the Keighley Free Church Council, too. After eighteen months of fruitless protests to the long-suffering MP, plus a petition of 1,719 signatures, it was 'suggested that the point be raised with Mr Lees-Smith whether the government was afraid to act in this matter for fear of offending the working people who might refuse to work if they did not get their usual quantities of beer'. Fortunately, wiser counsels observed 'that this would amount to a kind of slander on the workers'.

The minutes of Keighley Free Church Council meetings – once its members had thrashed out the vexed question of their official representation at civic functions – reveal what now seems a well-meaning naivety, but one in which they were by no means unique. They were troubled by 'the treatment of new recruits in the Army and the prevalence of swearing, which was contrary to Mr Eden's injunction to men entering the Army to "fear God"'. Presumably it was an old soldier among them who pointed out that 'swearing and cursing when giving orders' was indeed against Army regulations, which were however 'often extremely difficult to enforce'.

Another worry was 'the use of the Mechanics' Institute for dances and the accompanying sale of intoxicants with reference to the ill effect this could have on those who attended the place for educational purposes', to say nothing of the numbers of young people frequenting public houses. The Free Church Council proposed to conduct a census on this question, intriguingly finding some young people prepared to carry it out, but, like many another hotly debated issue, it seems to have remained simply a dusty item in a forgotten minute-book.

The Keighley Church of England Men's Society, struggling on with an inevitably reduced membership, discussed ways of helping the Forces and swore 'increased loyalty to the C.E.M.S. rule of life and ideals'. After an address by a Clayton curate on 'Evangelistic Opportunities during Wartime', members reached the (debatable) conclusion that 'young people during the blackout were often at a loss for suitable employment during leisure hours and would respond to evangelistic efforts'. When the Vicar of Holy Trinity spoke on 'The Work of an Army Chaplain' it was mysteriously agreed, at the speaker's request, 'that minutes of the address be not recorded'. Incidentally, Keighley certainly contributed towards the Forces' spiritual welfare. The Revd Edgar M.M. Bright, a former athletics champion at the Keighley Trade and Grammar School and future Superintendent Minister of the Keighley Methodist Circuit, was evacuated as an Army chaplain from Dunkirk; while the Revd F.J. Green, a former curate at St Mary's Church, Eastwood, went ashore as a chaplain on the D-Day beaches. When Canon J.C.F. Hood left Iceland he became Deputy-Assistant Chaplain General in the South of England. In 1945 his successor as Rector of Keighley was the Revd Eric Treacy, another senior chaplain attached to the British Liberation Army.

Chapter Seven

'A Body of Disciplined and Interested Young Men'

Local school children – bearing in mind that they were not, in the main, physically endangered – had a relatively interesting war, as can be glimpsed in their head teachers' logbooks. In larger town schools, staffs of usually women teachers coped with classes of up to fifty pupils, occasionally more. Conditions could be cramped, evacuees, sometimes accompanied by their own teachers, exacerbating the problems. 'The Classroom for Class 4 is too small for 48 children,' complained the headmistress of Eastwood Council School. 'One desk fills up the passage leading to the door, making the exit and entrance very slow as children have to pass between the desk to get out.'

In the early months of the war the Bradford evacuees were a special source of concern. At Horkinstone Council School their own nurse visited regularly from Bradford to examine them, clothes for them were repeatedly delivered, and initially after the 1939 Christmas holidays only five out of twenty returned. In 1941 a boy left school in the middle of the afternoon and walked home to Bradford. Even some of the student teachers, who came periodically to gain classroom experience, had themselves been evacuated to Bingley from Edge Hill Training College at Liverpool.

Lessons were sometimes interrupted by air-raid shelter practices and ARP wardens checking gas masks (it was necessary to exchange some for larger sizes). Although in reality daytime sirens were rare, at least two headmistresses noted Keighley's first night warning in 1940. 'The first air-raid warnings were given during the night, June 19–20,' recorded the Holycroft Council School log. 'No bombs were dropped near here – this is the second large-scale attack on England.'

At Horkinstone Council School, Oxenhope, this had a sequel: 'An Air-Raid alarm was given last night and many of the children had been awakened. From 1.30 p.m. to 2 p.m. Juniors and Infants were allowed to lie down and rest.'

Presumably Oxenhope was not regarded as a high air-raid risk, as all that the Horkinstone School had received by way of emergency equipment, late in

1939, was a stirrup-pump with a broken handle. 'A porter from the station' came and put it right. When it required a new tube in 1942 'Mr Jackson A.R.P. Warden fixed it'. Additionally, early in 1941 a man from the County Council delivered eight sandbags for use in the event of incendiary bombs.

A daytime warning on 1 April 1941 was meticulously chronicled at Ingrow Church of England School: 'This afternoon at 3.27 the siren sounded and the children were taken to the shelter. The "All-clear" was sounded at 4.5 p.m. so the children were brought back into school for prayers, and then sent home.'

That same warning – according to caretaker and indefatigable Special Constable Robert Smith Williams – sent Steeton schoolchildren rushing home, though he noted 'more method at the Infants'. Another, on Easter Monday, caught him cleaning at Steeton Council School. 'There did not appear to be anything about,' he laconically recorded, 'so, like George Formby, I went on window cleaning'.

There were other disruptions. The blackout caused a rearranging of school hours, the winter timetable running from 9.30 a.m. to 12.15 p.m. and from 1.15 to 3.45 p.m., 'to enable children to get home before dark'. Schools closed for the first week of the war and allowed two days' holiday when Germany surrendered. On the other hand, they reopened, by order of the Board of Education, on Whit Tuesday in 1940 during what should have been a week's holiday 'owing to the extension of the war and the renewed threats of aerial bombardment'. Instructions were issued over the wireless: at Eastwood School all the staff and 61 per cent of the pupils responded, 72 per cent at Holycroft.

Education authority responsibilities increased as the war progressed. The Ingrow Church of England School log records the visit, early in 1942, of one of His Majesty's Inspectors 'to enquire how many children we had whose mothers went out to work'. It was 1944 before school dinners were introduced there – when twenty-one children, the head teacher, the caretaker and a helper availed themselves – but in larger schools they were being served by February 1942. Some 200 children at Holycroft ate school dinners on their first day, 132 at Eastwood.

Opening Holycroft during the summer holidays as a centre providing meals and milk was not, however, a success. Only three pupils said they wanted the service, and in the event only one turned up. Eastwood, on the other hand, where '44 children's mothers are out at work all day', fared much better, attracting seventy-three 'whose parents wish them to attend during the holidays', of whom twenty-nine stayed for dinner.

Wartime winters in the Pennines were severe, with much snow. On 6 March 1942 only nine pupils managed to struggle into rural Horkinstone School. Eastwood, a town school, mustered only 139 out of 224 on 29 January 1940; schools subsequently closed for several days. School nurses' visits of inspection

24 May was enthusiastically celebrated as Empire Day, when schools held special assemblies and pageants traditionally emphasising 'personal service and devotion to duty'. These children at Worth Village Primary School have formed a simple patriotic tableau, probably in an earlier year of the war. *(Mrs Freda Pickering)*

were regular and assiduous, and the occasional non-delivery of school milk was deemed 'a very serious loss'. Notwithstanding there were outbreaks of measles, whooping cough, chickenpox, mumps and scabies. During the latter half of the war, teachers' absences also tended to increase. The Holycroft headmistress was not untypical in 1945:

Jan. 9, 10 and 11. I have been away three days with a severe cold.
Jan. 15. I was again absent – 1½ days.

Jan. 24. Miss Langton is away also, today.
Jan. 29. Miss Carr absent – sick.

That same winter her Horkinstone counterpart had to take eleven days off with mumps, and the Ingrow headmaster was absent in April with a septic foot.

Attempts were made to bolster the food ration. One day in 1943 the Horkinstone children 'were provided with raw carrots to eat after dinner', and the headmistress was repeatedly issued with orange juice and cod liver oil for her under-5s. Christmas parties could sometimes run to jellies and biscuits. At Horkinstone, one Christmas, 'each child received two sixpenny stamps and one ounce of sweets (for which they each gave a D coupon)'.

Wartime circumstances meant extra hazards, especially where adjacent moors were used for military training. 'Two policemen called', worried the Horkinstone log in 1944, 'to ask some boys who had been to the shooting range, where the ammunition was'. Next day a policeman 'took empty cases etc.'. Two Holycroft schoolboys were killed in Lund Park in 1944 by the explosion of a 2in mortar bomb they were tampering with – it had been found on a trip to Harden Moor 'to collect shrapnel'. Another boy described being blown off his bicycle as 'like lifting him up in the air', and several bystanders were injured by splinters. The inquest heard disturbing evidence about 'a common practice for boys to go to the moor to see what they could find'. An Inspecting Ordnance Officer thought 'that certain safety devices incorporated in the design of the bomb had been negatived by the boys when they were playing with it'.

The wartime moors could indeed be dangerous, not least for the soldiers training there. The sun's heat was to explode a phosphorous oil incendiary bomb on Ilkley Moor ten years after the war. A second lieutenant and sergeant of the Idle Home Guard were killed on Hallas Moor by a premature explosion in the breech of a gun they were demonstrating. A Regular lance-sergeant died in a mortar accident on Ilkley Moor. A major supervising an exercise was shot dead near Silsden by a lance-corporal who had inadvertently got a live round mixed in with his blanks.

Sadly, warning notices around prohibited areas failed to prevent irresponsible behaviour. In 1945 three teenage boys and a girl were hurt on Harden Moor when they threw a mortar-bomb against a wall. A few weeks later a 13-year-old was killed and another badly injured; the dead boy's mackintosh pocket was full of mortar-bomb fins.

The war nonetheless also exerted a positive influence. Children were taught to save. 'Mr Scribner called p.m. to explain the working of the Savings Association Group,' wrote the Horkinstone headmistress early in 1940. 'We started our group today.' By 1944 this modest school (a wintry '17 children present out of 43' gives an idea of numbers) was contributing £100 0s 2d towards Salute the Soldier Week. Holycroft's School War Savings Association netted £175 in its first five months. By mid-1941 pupils' savings averaged £34 13s per week, and a special effort to raise £100 to pay for two Bren guns closed at £143 4s. Their Warship Week total was £700, Wings for Victory Week £1,037 2s, and Salute the Soldier Week £1,300 6s. A 'Raise the Standard' War Savings Campaign late in 1943 brought the percentage of Holycroft savers up to 99.5 per cent. Even when the war was over, during Thanksgiving Week in 1945 the school saved £1,201 7s. Of course, children were encouraged. Local George Medal recipient Kenneth Bland of the RAF addressed the Holycroft scholars in 1943 about the importance of War Savings. The Eastwood log catalogues visits by 'the National Savings outdoor Cinema' showing a 'propaganda film' (the word was then used unselfconsciously). Eastwood pupils featured in the activities of Warship and other special Weeks.

These could be exciting. Horkinstone children made models for a Warship Week exhibition, the headmistress taking three boys into town by taxi in order to arrange them. The top class from the Ingrow Church of England School marched in 'a procession from the Car Park in Bridge Street to the Town Hall Square. Here they were addressed by the Director of Education for Bradford'; the Infants were given a holiday instead. Classes 2 and 3 at Holycroft performed *Peter Pan* in aid of Wings for Victory Week; the chairman of the Education Committee visited school afterwards to congratulate them on their efforts. Oakworth Council School put on 'a miniature military display' in Holden Park, in which 'well-known songs were parodied to refer to the savings scheme'. Twenty-four children from Eastwood contributed 'a group of songs' to a Schools' Festival, which required a rehearsal in the impressive Municipal Hall. During Salute the Soldier Week Class 4 sang four songs at a Children's Festival Concert: they were 'Cherry Ripe', 'Now Is the Month of Maying', 'Summer is A-Coming In', and 'Care Flies from the Lad that is Merry'.

Wartime children, thanks to the war effort and the obvious needs of others, turned their hands to many things. They knitted blanket squares for hospitals

Wings for Victory Week, 1943: children from Oakworth Council School in Holden Park present their 'musical parody of War Savings', in which 'well-known songs were parodied to refer to the savings scheme'. *(Mrs M.C. Prewett)*

(Holycroft had finished sixteen by Christmas 1939), and collected waste and silver paper, tins, and acorns for pig-keepers. In July 1940 Eastwood specialised in 'aluminium goods not needed' and sent off a lorry-load 'for making aeroplanes'. Before Christmas they held a 'Santa Claus' assembly to which pupils brought toys and books for Toc H to distribute to poorer children.

They gave concerts galore, in aid of the Red Cross, the local Comforts Fund, the Soldiers', Sailors' and Airmen's Families Association. They contributed 'a surprising quantity of goods' on Hospital Pound Day – '3 hampers full' at Holycroft in 1943. On Empire Days, celebrated with special assemblies and the chorusing of hymns, songs and National Anthems, they held collections for the Over-Seas Tobacco League, which in the case of Holycroft provided cigarettes for the crew of HMS *Porcupine*, while in 1942 Eastwood sent '60 parcels each containing 50 cigarettes to members of Forces serving abroad'.

They certainly understood the meaning of Armistice Day, duly commemorated with two minutes' silence. On the third anniversary of the outbreak of the war, the Horkinstone headmistress took her older pupils to Oxenhope Church for a National Day of Prayer service.

Ironically, the war offered extra educational opportunities and helped broaden children's horizons. Some Keighley classes attended matinée performances of *Where the Rainbow Ends* in 1942. When the famous Lanchester Marionette Theatre of Malvern, touring under ENSA, gave a show in 1943 the local branch of the National Association of Head Teachers arranged for four additional performances, which were attended by 1,400 Keighley children and teachers; profits went to the St John Ambulance Brigade Nursing Division. Dame Sybil Thorndike, appearing in *Jacob's Ladder* at the Hippodrome, gave a Saturday-morning talk to the upper forms of the Boys' and Girls' Grammar Schools and the City of London School for Girls.

Horkinstone Juniors listened to a topical broadcast on Iceland in 1941, and two Canadian soldiers told them about Canada. The Boys' Grammar School – with an eye to potential recruiting – had talks on the Army, the RAF and the Fleet Air Arm, with repeated film-shows by the Ministry of Information. At the Junior Technical School Denis Healey, the Principal's son, dressed in khaki and fresh from a trouble spot, lectured the City of London Girls' School on Greece. 'I complained next day that I was stiff,' one of his listeners was to recall, 'having had to sit on the floor for an hour and forty minutes'.

Flight Lieutenant Arthur Feeley, former pupil and choirboy of St Anne's Roman Catholic School, paid a visit in 1943 after being awarded the Distinguished Flying Cross for navigating on 'a large number of operational sorties, attacking many of the enemy's most heavily defended targets in Germany'. The St Anne's pupils presented him with a clock and a wallet, and entertained him with songs and selections from *HMS Pinafore*. Thanking them,

Flight Lieutenant Arthur Feeley, DFC, visiting his old school at St Anne's, Keighley, in 1943. The children presented him with a clock and a wallet, and entertained him with songs, including a selection from *HMS Pinafore*. (*Mr Edwin Murgatroyd*)

he modestly and significantly remarked 'that the school should share in any honour that he might have gained, for the two strongest influences of his life had been those of his home and his school'.

Eastwood Council School took exceptional advantage of current conditions. In December 1941 Class 4 had talks on Christmas in Czechoslovakia by 'Dr Reidl, refugee' and Christmas in Spain by 'Senorita Carmen Ramos, refugee from The Basque Country' (Senorita Ramos, who was from Bilbao, subsequently joined the staff but, after repeated absences, died in 1945).

Warrant Officer A. Legge of the RAF, 'who has lived 6 years in India and been in charge of Broadcasting House Bombay, for 2 years, gave an interesting talk on India'. Life in Singapore was described in 1942 by a Mrs Moore, 'who has recently returned to England after having spent 20 years' there; and Madagascar by the Revd A.M. Churgwin, 'an authority on the subject, having broadcast after the news on May 5 when our forces attacked and took over the North of the Island'. Repatriated prisoner of war Corporal Sharman talked about his experiences, while Squadron Leader R.A. Butler, DSO, DSC, flew the flag for National Savings in Thanksgiving Week.

Mindful also of the children's physical well-being, the Keighley Elementary Education Subcommittee tried to keep open their Humphrey Head Camp School, near Kents Bank on the shores of Morecambe Bay. Week by week for the previous thirty years this 'very suitable wooden building of pleasing appearance' had provided healthy summer breaks for alternate batches of boys and girls, who interspersed lessons with periods outside 'in the sunshine and wind' until townie faces became brown and sunburnt. In 1941 children were to be allowed 'free use of the Second Class Slipper Bath on the Saturday morning prior to their visit'.

Alas, barely had the first 1941 batch arrived at this idyllic spot than the area was bombed. The children spent a disturbed night out of doors and were returned to Keighley the following morning, members of the Keighley Rotary Club ferrying them from the station to their respective homes. The camp, having suffered £50-worth of damage by enemy action, was closed for the duration, although William Hulme's Grammar School at Manchester, being of sterner stuff, promptly requested its use during the summer holidays 'for the purpose of billeting boys from that school who have volunteered to go to the Grange district to work on the land'. Keighley lent them the camp for a nominal rent of a guinea a week.

The Boys' Grammar School camp at Kirkcudbright was also discontinued, some pupils finding other outlets for their spare time. 'Since we broke up for the Summer Holidays', observed the school magazine in 1940, 'a considerable number of boys in the Upper School have joined the Home Guard, and at least one of the masters is a member in the Keighley Group. There are several masters and boys, too, in the A.R.P.' The headmaster notified the War Agricultural Executive Committee of over sixty senior pupils who were willing to help with farm work during their summer holidays, though only 'one or two' local farmers took up the offer. Notwithstanding, they offered their services again the following year.

The demands of the Home Front involved young people in other positive activities. Keighley No. 100 Squadron of the Air Training Corps was formed in 1939, aiming at 'the creation of a body of disciplined and interested young men who, on completion of their training, would be of immediate service in the event of a crisis'. Within weeks, the squadron had found headquarters at Royd Works and paraded fifty cadets on its first inspection; soon they were camping and gliding at Kirbymoorside.

Two years later its new Cavendish Street headquarters in the former United Methodist Free Church was equipped with a 16hp Flying Flea engine, a bomb sight and camera gun turret, bomb racks and a parachute, and even for a while a DH Puss Moth light aeroplane lent by an Apperley Bridge resident whose flight lieutenant son, its owner, had been killed. The Air Ministry supplied a 14-cylinder Jaguar radial aircraft engine. Cadets learned wireless and Morse code, fired on a miniature rifle range and practised repairing fabric on wing sections. During weekends and evenings they did squad drill and physical training in Lund and Victoria Parks. Their training included flights from 'a Northern Air Station'.

The Keighley unit developed what was thought to be the only Air Training Corps choir in the country, which broadcast in 1944 in a programme called *First Flights*. Thirty-five of its excited members went to London to be recorded alongside Arthur Askey, 'Stinker' Murdoch and the Billy Cotton Band. They sang 'We Are the Sons of the Lords of the Air', a specially arranged version of 'She'll Be Coming Round the Mountain' and (echoes now of a long-gone era) 'Ma, I Miss Your Apple Pie'.

Keighley Army Cadet Corps enrolled its first seventy boys in 1942, lagging slightly behind a St Anne's Roman Catholic company and a Silsden unit already under initiation, by a Home Guard sergeant-major and two sergeants, into the complexities of squad drill, foot drill, weapons instruction and field tactics. During Parish Feast weeks Army Cadets joined big West Riding camps at Denton Park, near Ilkley.

The Keighley St Anne's Girls' Training Corps and Boys' Cadet Corps on parade on Sunday 25 October 1942, near the Roman Catholic chapel – the future Our Lady of Victories – at Guard House. After a service the Right Revd Monsignor Russell, seen on the left, took the salute. *(Mr J. McGlinchey)*

Leaders and cadets of the Keighley Girls' Training Corps, the 329th such company to be formed, in 1942. *(Mrs Ryder)*

The Girls' Training Corps formed its 329th company in Keighley in 1942, again preceded by one at St Anne's, which ran an Evening Institute offering instruction in such useful subjects as shorthand and typing, book-keeping, cookery, needlework and first aid. Sponsored by the Youth Council, this was intended for 'the masses of girls who have not shared in the life of the community since they left school at the age of fourteen', and claimed an 'all-pervading ideal of preparing the girls for the duties of Christian citizenship'.

At a time when young women were liable for conscription into the Armed Forces or war work, however, there was an emphasis on pre-service training. Some girls attended special courses at the Technical College, including one on preparation for joining the Women's Auxiliary Air Force; others joined a knitting group in aid of the Russians. Their first anniversary in 1943 was marked by a route march through town, followed by displays of marching and drill, when the chairman of their Administration Committee took the opportunity of making a public appeal for spare clothing coupons to enable the girls to acquire woollen blouses for the winter.

The Keighley Sea Cadet Corps was commissioned in 1943 and named its headquarters after the town's adopted HMS *Marne*, which later presented its namesake with a German bugle captured in the Aegean. When the cadets toured HMS *Marne* itself in 1944 they were 'even allowed to operate the power-turret guns' and admired the Keighley coat-of-arms mounted in a place of honour over the wardroom mantelpiece.

The Keighley Youth Council, offspring of a West Riding County Youth Committee formed at the request of the Board of Education in 1941, made itself responsible 'for the welfare of young people between the ages of 14 and 20'; its aims were 'the provision of healthy and profitable recreation for young people of both sexes'. Essentially to begin with this meant sport – the County Council paid for the services of 'a fully qualified instructor in physical training' one night a week – but also attempted were a wider range of activities, debates, dramatics, singing, music, ballroom and country dancing.

Indeed, the Youth Council formed the basis for the youth clubs that were to survive the war by decades. Youth groups were started in every district, though one at Oakworth experienced trouble finding premises when the proposed school 'was of a modern design with a large expanse of glass which would require blacking out at considerable expense'. Youngsters were conducted on tours of works and factories, and encouraged to go rambling and to get

The 5th Keighley Guide Company formed up before a wartime procession, probably in November 1940, prior to a British Legion service at Keighley Parish Church. *(Enid White)*

interested in organisations like the St John Ambulance Brigade. A Fitness for Service class for girls soon attracted seventy members.

A Spiritual Welfare Subcommittee kept an eye on moral issues, discussing the advisability of lecturers from the British Social Hygiene Council, deploring fund-raising by 'a method known as "raffling"' and resolving 'that this Council recognises the value of our English Sunday, and desires the various Leaders of the Youth Groups not to arrange organised games on Sundays'.

Chapter Eight

'More Jam, More Jam, More Jam, More Jam'

The changing moods of the Second World War can be broadly measured by the bill of fare at Keighley's Hippodrome or New Queen's Theatre – which still went by both names although officially it had been the Hippodrome since 1909.

The Hippodrome represented popular culture and recreation. 'We would hurry from work in the evenings', one habitué was to recall, 'and join in the long queues for the pit or the gallery. Inside the orchestra was tuning up, and everywhere there was the general air of excitement, waiting for the moment the curtain rose.'

To begin with, the 'Phoney War' period was characterised by such comedy revues as *Why Be Serious?* and *Let's Be Merry*, *Brighter Nights* and *Just Nuts*. The titles suggest that many adopted a light-hearted approach to the war itself: *Black Out the Blues*, *Laugh for Victory*, *Eyes Front*, *Blue Pencil Revue* (a dig at the censor), *Sh—— Keep It Dark*, *We're in the Army Now*. There were risqué offerings, too, the likes of which a rather dour West Riding town had probably never seen before: *Silk Stocking Scandals*, *Show a Leg*, *Stars and Strips*, *Don't Be Shy* and *Capers and Sauce*. *Soir de Paris* was 'Fast! Saucy! Oo-la-la!', while *Nuit de Joie* featured 'the lovely night of joy girls' and *Oh! You Girls!* had 'Harry Roy's sex appeal glamour girls'. Casts included names then or soon to become well known, like Joe King and Bunny Doyle, and Donald Peers and Beryl Reid in supporting roles.

From the midsummer of 1940 the famous were to become increasingly familiar in the provinces as the bombing of London and major cities, the necessity for boosting public morale and the efforts of a national Council for the Encouragement of Music and the Arts brought the theatrical and cultural top drawer to towns like Keighley. Before 1940 was out the Hippodrome had played host to Reginald Foort and his Mighty Organ, Billy Scott-Coomber and his Singing Grenadiers, Albert Modley and his New Variety Road Show (a repeated visitor) and Carroll Levis's BBC Discoveries.

Keighley's Queen's Theatre or Hippodrome ('Queen's Theatre' is carved across the frontage, while letters spelling 'Hippodrome' appear vertically down its left-hand side). The

space in the foreground had been cleared for the bus station offices opened in 1940.
(Keighley Reference Library)

Henry Hall's Guest Night was broadcast from the second house on Friday, 20 September.

By 1941 Keighley was enjoying theatrical treats as never before: Joe Loss, Jack Payne and Oscar Rabin; Sid Field, Norman Evans, Jimmy James and Company, Sandy Powell and his Road Show; the Western Brothers, Cavan O'Connor ('Radio's most romantic personality'), Rawicz and Landauer ('a thrill on two pianos'), Issy Bonn ('Radio's Famous Hebrew Comedian'), and G.H. Elliott, 'the famous chocolate-coloured coon'. Rob Wilton appeared as 'Mr Muddlecombe, JP' and Charlie Kunz shared the stage with Wee Georgie Wood and Stainless Stephen. There were also musicals – *Lilac Time* and *No, No, Nanette* – and the bands of the Leicestershire and the Duke of Wellington's Regiments. For the higher-brow the Sadler's Wells Opera gave *La Traviata*, *Dido and Aeneas* and *The Marriage of Figaro*.

The following year saw Frank Randle in *Randle's Scandals* and a reflection of America's entry into the war with *Yankee Doodle Comes to Town*, but mainly the emphasis was on culture. In a single, breathless week the Royal Carl Rosa Opera Company performed *Madam Butterfly*, *Rigoletto*, *Faust*, *Die Fledermaus*, *La Bohème*, *Il Travatore* and *The Barber of Seville*. The touring Old Vic Theatre presented Laurence Housman's *Jacob's Ladder*, starring Sybil Thorndike and Lewis Casson, while a Russian revue, *Moscow Belle*, featured dancer Tamara Desni and Polish violinist Jan Korski. There were Russian and Anglo-Polish Ballets, and Italia Conti's patriotic extravaganza *Where the Rainbow Ends* (featuring St George for England in his silver armour vanquishing the evil dragon) came twice, late in 1942 and again in 1943.

By that time quality plays dominated the winter months. The repertoire of Harry Hanson's Court Players included *When We Are Married*, *Hobson's Choice*, *Dangerous Corner*, *The Corn is Green*, *Pygmalion*, *Blithe Spirit* and *Night Must Fall*. The Old Vic returned with John Drinkwater's *Abraham Lincoln* and – appropriately for the locality – a drama based on Charlotte Brontë's *Shirley*. Similarly, film star Mary Morris appeared in *Wuthering Heights*, and Tod Slaughter in the melodrama *Maria Marten, or The Murder in the Red Barn*.

Plays were also the norm in 1944, thanks to the Court Players, the Famous Manchester Repertory Company, and Phillip Barrett and Eileen Herlie from the West End: *Rebecca*, *Recipe for Murder*, *East Lynne*, *Yellow Sands*, *Mrs Warren's Profession* . . . but a more relaxed mood in early 1945 saw the return of Albert Modley and comedy revues. *We Were in the Forces* that April had 'a cast of over 30 artists, discharged from H.M. Forces'!

Attractions overflowed the Hippodrome into the Municipal Hall and the Ritz Cinema. The Council for the Encouragement of Music and the Arts (or CEMA – its aims were 'to bring music or any of the arts to those places which normally found it difficult to obtain them') sent the Ukrainian pianist Lev Pouishnov to play Chopin and Liszt at a rather unpromising time of day. 'It was a great pity', the local press aptly commented, 'that a concert by so brilliant an artist should have been held on a Monday afternoon when so many people were unable to avail themselves of an opportunity never likely to recur.' At least secondary schools were encouraged to send classes along. Happily, when the Russian pianist Moiseiwitsch came, at his own expense under the auspices of Mrs Churchill's Aid to Russia Fund, with a programme of Beethoven, Schumann and Brahms in 1945, he was able to attract a large audience.

The Market Theatre of the Rural Entertainment Society – again sponsored by CEMA – drew a full house in the Girls' Grammar School when giving Shaw's *Dark Lady of the Sonnets* and Housman's *Victoria Regina*, throwing in for good measure a versatile mixture of guitar and eighteenth-century songs, sea shanties, yodelling and a Strauss polka. CEMA was again responsible for Patrick Ludlow and his London company presenting A.A. Milne's *Michael and Mary* at the Hippodrome, Patrick Ludlow having recently appeared with Flanagan and Allen in the film *We'll Smile Again*.

Meanwhile the Ritz Cinema organ was used for a Grand Concert by Flying Officer Reginald Dixon, 'Famous Broadcasting Organist from the Tower, Blackpool', accompanied by the East Yorkshire Regimental Band. Other notables came to talk. Late in 1943 a Keighley Anglo-Soviet Society arranged for the Dean of Canterbury to speak on 'Russia, Our Ally'. The Fabian Society invited Dr C.E.M. Joad of the BBC *Brains Trust*, who addressed a crowded Municipal Hall one winter Sunday afternoon on 'The Future of Education'; he came again for a *Brains Trust* in 1944. Novelist Bernard Newman spoke on 'How Goes the War' in 1941, and Lieutenant Kathleen de Villiers, of the South African WAAF but better-known as Field Marshal Smuts's adopted daughter, attended a social in aid of the Oakworth Soldiers', Sailors' and Airmen's Association.

There is even an oral tradition of Bing Crosby crooning on Keighley railway station to a train-full (some versions say two trains-full) of American troops en route to or from Scotland!

The cinema was quick to exploit wartime moods. Before September 1939 was out, the Regent Picture House was screening *Let Freedom Ring*, billed as 'a pulse-stirring drama of the fight for freedom'. The following month it showed *Devil and the Deep* – 'the thrilling story of a submarine commander's jealousy of his wife' – while a December offering at the Picture House was *The Spy in Black* or 'the story of U-boat 29'.

More famously perhaps, January 1940 opened with *The Lion Has Wings* at the Regent, a 'Terrific Epic of the R.A.F.' starring Ralph Richardson and Merle Oberon, and ostensibly 'depicting the part being played in the present conflict with Germany by the British Air Force'. A week later it was on again at the Oxford Hall, this time hailed as 'the Romance of the R.A.F.' and 'Britain's Reply to Hitler's Challenge'.

The ubiquitous wireless was used to broaden provincial horizons. A programme called *Back Home* was broadcast from Haworth in 1942, featuring a farmer, a weaver, the Brontë Museum curator, the conductor of the Bridgehouse Methodist choir and the secretary of the Haworth Public Prize Band. Sadly, however, when Keighley got mentioned on a *Brains Trust* transmission late in 1941, the questionmaster's mispronunciation of the name as 'Keely' sent what the *Yorkshire Evening News* exaggeratedly called 'a cold shiver' through Keighley radio listeners!

Indeed, culture in its broadest sense ripened during the war. In his 1939 annual report, Chief Librarian Thomas J. Kirkpatrick had highlighted the demand for what he called 'crisis' books, such as Lockhart's *Guns or Butter*, Gadye's *Fallen Bastions* and Eden's *Foreign Affairs*. There was considerable interest in the unexpurgated edition of Hitler's *Mein Kampf*, while characters in the most popular novel, *Gone With the Wind*, were shown notably coping with an earlier war. He predicted that 'reading will increase, and libraries will become a very important service in the lives of the people during wartime'.

In this he was proved resoundingly correct. Membership of Keighley Public Library had risen from 3,887 in 1939 to 14,162 by 1946. Annual reports were a minor casualty of the Second World War, but statistics were kept for later publication: total book issues from central and branch libraries rose from 144,228 in 1939 to 524,024 in 1945. Mr Kirkpatrick, however, did not oversee this increase. When he was called up into the RAF in 1941 his predecessor came back out of retirement. Robert S. Crossley had started his career in 1887 as assistant at the old Mechanics' Institute library, becoming Keighley's first Borough Librarian in 1904. Now he was to continue in harness until 1946.

On the other hand, war posed problems for libraries. The banning from the reading room in 1940 of *Peace News*, the official organ of the Peace Pledge Union, called forth accusations of 'violating and outraging one of the fundamentals of English liberty'. The Communist *Daily Worker* followed suit but was reinstated in 1943, presumably owing to the Soviet Union's having become an ally.

As the winter of 1942 drew in, the reading room had to close on Sundays because of fuel restrictions. The increase in library users itself posed a problem of 'severe congestion' for which the Town Council found a draconian solution, resolving that 'the Children's Library be closed until such time as other suitable accommodation can be provided and that the space vacated be added to the existing Lending Library'. It did not re open until 1948.

The Reference Library doubled as an art gallery when, in 1941, the British Institute of Adult Education organised an 'Art for the People' exhibition of watercolours and drawings by contemporary artists illustrating developments over the previous forty years, which persuaded Rotary Club members to forgo for once their weekly after-lunch address in favour of pondering the challenges of Cubism and Surrealism. The Lord Beaverbrook Collection of Russian Photographs was topically displayed there in 1942, as were – for the benefit of allotment-holders – illustrations from the Royal Horticultural Society on how to grow vegetables. Factory workers' art followed in 1944.

Home-made entertainment flourished. True, *Betty*, the planned 1939 production of the Keighley Amateur Operatic and Dramatic Society, had to be cancelled (it had in any case run into difficulties, not least the show's need for a live cockatoo!), and the Amateurs as an organisation went into abeyance until 1946; but some of its members became more active than ever.

In 1940 the Military Entertainments Officer at Whitby requested 'that the members of the Society give a Variety Concert for the troops at the Spa Theatre'; profits went in aid of the Royal Signals Comforts Fund, while the Society's expenses included such engaging items as 'coffee at Malton', 'wigs from Hombergs', and 'petrol for 2 cars carrying the Nig-Nog Troupe'. Thereafter the Amateurs, in company with Lewis Scargill's Gresham Players, were in great demand for entertaining the Forces. A careful press, anxious not to locate military concentrations, mysteriously chronicled their expeditions to 'an East Coast town', 'a Northern town' and 'stations far removed from Keighley'.

Concert party fare was not always of the subtlest. 'This was just the usual E.N.S.A. type show,' a Keighley aircraftman tellingly wrote home from the Orkneys in 1941:

I learnt the other day that owing to the smallness of the island we only get the, shall we say, 'second-rate' parties. In all the shows there's always the community singing, the pianist who plays 'Daisy' the same as Bach, Gershwin or Beethoven would have played it, etc. Still, they provide a break and we usually get a laugh when the 'oomph' girl of the troupe makes love to the officers! The concert in this case was given by 'The Four Smart Girls', one of them as it happens was a girl, the other three were nearer the 40 mark, for all that though they worked really hard and gave quite a decent show.

A sample from the manuscript repertoire of a Keighley concert party evokes the homeliness of their entertainment:

At Number Three next door to me
The lady takes in boarders.
She's as sweet as sweet can be,
And so say all the boarders.
Jam and bread is all they get,
But still they don't complain.
When they all sit down to tea
You'll hear them all exclaim:

Chorus:

'More jam, more jam, more jam, more jam,
Don't want beef with mustard,
Don't want fruit with custard.
What's the stuff they give the troops
To fill their diaphragm? —
More jam, more jam, more jam, more jam!'

Rude jingles between turns could bring the proverbial house down:

Hitler, no doubt, when his life gives out,
Will ride in a fiery chariot,
And sit in state on a red-hot plate,
With the Devil and Judas Iscariot.

or:

I wish I were a little bird
To fly from place to place.
I'd settle on Herr Hitler's nose
Then tread all over his face.

The word carefully written in the repertoire book is indeed 'tread', although depending on the disposition of the audience alternatives could be plucked from a wide vocabulary of bodily functions!

One especially noteworthy Keighley concert party was The Good Companions (they had to get J.B. Priestley's permission to use the name), in which the future television comedienne Mollie Sugden learnt her trade as a young 'recitalist'. Other members were tenor Frank Smith, soprano Hylda Saville-Smith, baritone Arthur Day and pianist Walter Greenwood. During a three-year period The Good Companions gave some 500 shows, many under

A young Mollie Sugden – Keighley's future star of television comedy – sits second from the right as 'recitalist' with The Good Companions in 1942. This Keighley concert party gave 500 shows in a three-year period. Its other members were, from left to right, Frank Smith, tenor; Hylda Saville-Smith, soprano; Arthur Day, baritone; and Walter Greenwood, pianist. *(Mr E. O'Brien)*

the auspices of Northern Command at Catterick, and at an RAF station at Kirkburton. Sometimes they arrived back home at 3 a.m. – and Mollie Sugden had to be up early to work at the Steeton Royal Ordnance Factory. When Frank Smith's young son was taken along, he recalls being sick after being treated in officers' messes to delicacies unfamiliar to his rationed stomach!

Chapter Nine

'A Record the School Should be Proud of'

Week by week from 1940 onwards the *Keighley News* published a column of small print and tiny photographs headed variously 'Local Roll of Honour', 'War Casualties' or 'Toll of the War'; and week by week somebody in the Reference Library cut them out and pasted them into a scrapbook, whose concentrated and cumulative effects are sad indeed.

One early casualty was Captain William Gay Burdett of Peacehaven, Sussex, reported missing, believed killed, who had since 1937 been the prospective Conservative candidate for the Keighley Parliamentary Division. Haworth's first death, Sapper Thomas Clay, a 34-year-old father of three, was killed in France the day after returning from leave.

Canon J.C.F. Hood, Rector of Keighley, lost his only son, Lieutenant John Kennedy Hood of the Rifle Brigade, who was killed in North Africa. Pilot Officer Christopher Mark Handley, younger son of the Revd Thomas Handley, Vicar of St Peter's Church, Halifax Road, having flown forty-seven operational flights, went missing on his last before being grounded.

Driver Frank Thompson, aged 22, had played football for Thwaites Brow and cricket for Long Lee. Flight Lieutenant Leslie Lawrence Whitaker, DFC, was reported missing in May 1944, but not until April of the following year was it learnt that he had died on night operations.

At the beginning of 1945 Lieutenant D. Malcolm Henderson, nephew of a former Mayor of Keighley, died with Admiral Sir Bertram Ramsay, Naval Commander-in-Chief of the Allied Expeditionary Force, in a plane crash near Paris.

Gunner Arthur Shaw was captured at the fall of Singapore. 'A few days after receiving a card from her husband saying that he was a prisoner of war and in excellent health,' runs a terse newspaper paragraph from September 1943, 'Mrs A. Shaw, of 24, Apsley Street, Keighley, has had a telegram informing her that her husband, Gnr Arthur Shaw, has died in a Thailand prison camp of beri-beri fever'.

Private Hedley Dixon of the Queen's Royal Regiment was sent to France in June 1944. 'We have just got washed and shaved in a cig. tin,' he informed his wife, 'and one of the lads asked me to save him a drop of the water, so you can tell what a laugh we are getting. Although we are sleeping under the hedges like a lot of sheep we are not doing too bad.' Sometimes he drew cats at the end of his letters, to amuse his young son and daughter. 'I can't tell you much as every day is alike here,' he wrote, but between censorship and his instinct to appear reassuring he was scarcely painting the full picture. 'Tell our Eric there is plenty of big bangs here.'

A bundle of letters Mrs Dixon had sent him was subsequently returned unopened (only one had reached him), for he was killed on 21 July. 'The battalion had just withdrawn after being relieved, and we were re-grouping for another attack in an area which was under spasmodic shell-fire,' a padre wrote to her. 'It was during one of these periods of shelling that Hedley was hit and died at once.' The padre had 'laid him to rest on the grassy bank by the side of the road'.

Audiences watching a newsreel at the Silsden Picture Palace spotted local painter and decorator Irwin Shackleton marching with the Durham Light Infantry. The cinema obligingly reran the reel for the benefit of Mrs Shackleton and his family. Irwin was killed in action in Italy in 1944.

'I couldn't believe it for a minute,' his sapper brother-in-law, who had recently met him out there, wrote home.

He was so full of life and good spirits it didn't seem possible. . . . He was confident that the war would soon be over and we would all be going home again, he was as proud as punch of our Myra & his wee Margaret, he showed me all the photos and snaps he had, he carried them in his breast pocket with his letters from home. His last words to me were, 'Well if I don't see thee again Keep Smiling & Best of Luck lad.'

'Yes Irwin did have some good pals, he always said he had,' his widow replied to a letter from his company lieutenant. 'Thanks for going back to him, you must have been in great danger yourself.'

In August 1945 medical orderly J.W. Downs was badly burned trying to save his patients when his Japanese prison camp caught fire during an Allied bombardment; he died five days before Japan surrendered. 'I could not possibly have had a better medical orderly,' wrote his commanding officer. 'He died for his comrades.'

Belgian brothers François and Victor Van Hooren had spent four years of their boyhood in Keighley as refugees in the First World War; later, as hotel proprietors in Blankenberge and Middlekerk, they had been popular with West Riding tourists in the International Brotherhood Alliance. Arrested by the

Gestapo in 1943 for involvement with the Underground Movement, both were executed in October 1944.

Wireless operator and air gunner Sergeant Gordon Bottomley had become a member of the Caterpillar Club by virtue of twice having had to bale out; he went missing over Germany in 1941, later reappearing as a prisoner of war.

In April 1944 several local radio hams picked up a message from Malaya sent by Dr D.W. Gillies, a Keighley practitioner serving as a major in the Royal Army Medical Corps and captured at Singapore: 'I am quite well. Treatment and quarters satisfactory. No need to worry. Hope you are all well and happy. Keep smiling. Long to see you again. Best love.'

Royal Marine Commando Jack Meegan, from Silsden, wounded in the right arm, the left leg and the neck during a raid on Tobruk, was awarded the Distinguished Service Medal (DSM).

There were many such honours. Lieutenant-Colonel R.S. Smith, MC, DCM, a hero from the First World War, had been head postmaster at Keighley for just one day before being called up in 1939; a year later, working in Air Formation Signals, he received an OBE 'for distinguished services in France'.

Former postman Robert Herbert Metcalfe, Royal Marine gun-layer, gained an OBE for bravery during an enemy raid on a home port. He regretted the loss of his favourite pipe, which had been in a pocket of the overcoat he had wrapped round an incendiary bomb before throwing it overboard!

Leading Aircraftman Kenneth Bland, aged 27, was awarded the George Medal as an armourer in a south of England airfield. Former colleagues at the Borough Treasurer's Department recalled him as 'a quiet unassuming young fellow', but his citation paints a more vivid picture:

In June, 1941, ammunition in an aircraft exploded by spontaneous combustion. In spite of the explosions Aircraftman Bland climbed on to the mainplane and unfastened the gun panels. By this time the ammunition tank was burning fiercely, so he released it from the gun. Leading Aircraftman Williams carried away the burning tank which started to explode while he was carrying it. The presence of mind and courage shown by these two airmen undoubtedly saved the aircraft, and probably the lives of the air crews and armourers who were emptying the remaining ammunition tanks.

Said Leading Aircraftman Bland: 'I only did what any other armourer would have done in similar circumstances.' Councillors and Town Hall staff subsequently subscribed towards a silver and ivory tea service in 'tangible recognition of his bravery'.

Second Officer Douglas Crook, 23, received the MBE for piloting twenty-three survivors from a stricken vessel 1,200 miles in an open boat. He later won

When students of the Keighley Boys' Grammar School – aided by three of their counterparts from the Girls' Grammar School – presented Shakespeare's *Twelfth Night* in March 1945, proceeds helped provide parcels for 561 'Old Boys' then serving in the Forces. *(Mr Maurice Pegg)*

the George Medal for staying on board his ship after it was torpedoed and thought to be sinking and bringing it to port, displaying 'great and sustained courage, and his resource and resolution saved a valuable ship and probably many lives'.

At their annual reunion dinner early in 1941 Old Boys of Keighley Boys' Grammar School 'stood in silence, in memory of one who was present at the 1940 reunion, Lieutenant T. Miller, who lost his life with the Fleet Air Arm'.

Throughout the war the Old Keighlians made determined efforts to trace all their former pupils in the Forces, who were made honorary members of the Old Boys' Association during their service. Term by term they were listed as deaths, distinctions and news: 'Pvte. J. Brook, who is P.o.W. in Germany, sent a message over the German Radio, "Don't worry, I'm O.K." ' By 1943 their reunion diners were remembering fourteen Old Boys who had died on active service. Whist drives and dances helped finance a Comforts Fund, while the School's Dramatic Society production of *Twelfth Night* in 1945 raised the wherewithal for parcels for 561 Old Boys.

At their 1945 reunion the President 'reminded his hearers that 604 old boys of Keighley Boys' Grammar School and six masters had served, or were serving, with the Forces. Thirty-three boys and one master had given their lives; twelve were missing; and eight were prisoners of war. That was a record the school should be proud of.' Sadly, more deaths were to follow.

On Remembrance Day 1951, when 11 November happened to fall on a Sunday, a simple, dignified ceremony took place in the Public Library foyer where, thanks to the efforts of a British Legion Appeals Committee, a bronze plaque mounted on light oak was unveiled and dedicated. The Earl of Scarborough, Lord Lieutenant of the West Riding, drew aside the Union Jack that covered the plaque, and the Rector, the Revd E.C. Hamer, his words relayed to the crowds in the Town Hall Square outside, intoned: 'In the faith of our Lord Jesus Christ we dedicate this memorial to the Glory of God and in memory of those from this town and borough who laid down their lives in the World War 1939–1945.'

The plaque bore 296 names, compiled, as the *Keighley News* explained, through 'advertisements in our columns for relatives to supply details of those who died'. The list was thought at the time to be as complete as possible, but this is extremely unlikely. Local churches and organisations had cooperated with information on their lost members, but few replies came from individuals. 'Those who lost dear ones', it had to be assumed, 'prefer to keep their grief, and their memories, to themselves'.

Chapter Ten
'The Victor's Crown'

Final 'stand-down' parades of the Home Guard were held in early December 1944. On a dismal Sunday afternoon four companies of the Keighley (27th West Riding) Battalion marched past a saluting-base in North Street, where Colonel Sir Donald Horsfall took the salute. Afterwards there were speeches in the Picture House, where the Battalion was congratulated on 'its exceedingly good record', and Colonel Bateman, the Officer Commanding, told 'those who were of middle age that that would probably be the last time they would have the honour of wearing the King's uniform on an official occasion'.

Less formal stand-down dinners and suppers followed. Captain Caswell, addressing 'B' Company of the Riddlesden and Morton section, observed that 'the many jokes which had been made about the Home Guard had been taken in good part', and he thought 'the Volkssturm wished they were as good as the Home Guard had been'.

The year 1945 saw a general relaxing of conditions. Having been granted a petrol allowance, the Keighley Rotary Club started a 'get-you-home' service for the benefit of overseas personnel arriving on leave, a drivers' rota operating from 9.30 p.m. until midnight. In April the Victoria Hospital came off the Emergency Hospital Scheme, and in May the relevant committee decided to revive Silsden Show later in the summer. When the Spencer Street British Restaurant announced its imminent closure there were protests and a petition to the Ministry of Food. On its last day Derek Thompson 'entertained the diners to 40 minutes of pianoforte music'.

Prisoners of war were starting to trickle back home. Lance-Bombardier George Durkin and Private Thomas Leslie Smith arrived together, having escaped from different German camps during the Russian advance. 'We made our way through heavy snow to the rear of the Russian lines,' Durkin recounted, 'dragging our kit on sledges we had made'. Smith had been in Poland, 'where he had a rough time working in coal mines'. He had kept a German pipe as a souvenir, together with a Russian cap and wooden spoon painted with flowers.

Trooper John Clure had lived in a cave for five months while trying to evade capture in Greece. Leading Aircraftman Albert Moore, who had worked in an

On a dismal Sunday afternoon in December 1944 four companies of the Keighley (27th West Riding) Battalion of the Home Guard held their final 'stand-down' parade. Here 'D' Company, commanded by Major Norman Feather, MC, marches past a saluting-base in North Street, where Colonel Sir Donald Horsfall, Deputy Section Commander, takes the salute. *(William Speight/Mr John Fox)*

enemy sugar beet factory and whose German guards had finally told him to 'go and find the Americans', got home a day later than expected and 'missed the crowd that had assembled to give him greeting'.

Private Herbert Manning, captured in Libya in 1942, had joined the partisans after Italy surrendered. He described the Italian partisans' food supply: 'We sometimes bought, and sometimes stole.' His parents had received no news of him for over two years.

Corporal George Jones, from Eastburn, had been captured at Boulogne in 1940 and had five years' experience of prison camps in Poland, Danzig and Bavaria. 'The men who were taken prisoner with him had no water,' ran his reported recollections, 'so he scouted round, but in the end they had to drink champagne'. He was repatriated in February, with the heartening news that 'the German people know they are well beaten, and want us to take over Germany so that we can feed them'. They were, he thought, 'scared stiff' of the Russians.

By spring 1945 Germany was patently about to collapse, but the problem with planning celebrations was that nobody could be sure when victory would

Keighley members of the Royal Observer Corps celebrate victory. They include at least five mill managers, a garage proprietor, a solicitor, a master printer, a jeweller and a tobacconist. Two were full-time Observers. *(William Speight/Keighley Reference Library)*

actually be. As early as March the Keighley and Craven Holiday Fellowship was discussing a victory dance, trying to make arrangements 'as far as possible in advance'. At any rate, they were able to vote 30s towards getting their decorations ready. In mid-April the Directors of Prince-Smith and Stells Ltd decided that on 'V Day' – whenever that should be – they would pay '£1 to each male employee over 21 years of age, and 10/- to each female employee and male employee under 21 years of age'.

The Keighley Borough Finance Committee was facing similar uncertainty in April. Members resolved that the Mayor and Council should attend a public thanksgiving service at the Parish Church 'on the Sunday following the official announcement of victory in Europe'. In the meantime the Borough Engineer was allowed £40 and asked to consider 'a scheme for the decoration of the Square and the Town Hall and other public buildings in the centre of the town'.

The full Council Meeting that approved these resolutions on 1 May opened with Councillors standing in silence in memory of the American President, Franklin D. Roosevelt. The Mayor spoke of his 'deeply-lamented' death and 'the irreparable loss thus sustained by all the free nations engaged in the present war'.

Haworth welcomes home a returned prisoner of war in front of the Brontë Parsonage, 28 May 1945. Twenty-two-year-old Flight Sergeant Irvin Dransfield, standing between his father and mother, had been released by the Russians that April. There had just been a wedding at the adjacent Haworth Church, so the ground is liberally sprinkled with confetti. The lady in the dark costume, clutching her handbag under her arm, was the bride's mother! *(Mrs Annie Dransfield)*

Then, suddenly, on 7 May, the war in Europe was over as the BBC announced Germany's surrender. VE-Day was set for the next day, a Tuesday. In 1943 Keighley had received the news of Italy's surrender 'soberly and quietly', although a flag was flown from the Town Hall and some radio listeners who had heard a 6 p.m. BBC bulletin had 'dashed outside and passed on the glad tidings to those who had satisfied themselves from the evening papers that there was nothing new in the news'. But 1945 was quite different.

Minute-books of the time give insights into what Keighley people were doing. The Keighley and District Mutual Plate Glass Insurance Society, for example, was having difficulty replacing breakages, 'owing to diversion of plate glass for use in London and Southern Counties Areas', while the Keighley and District Photographic Association experienced an unusual problem, now that they could take down their blackout fittings – they had to fit a bolt 'to the inner door of the first dark-room to avoid inconvenient entry by another member'.

For weeks local schools had been saying goodbye to their evacuees – three London pupils left Horkinstone Council School in April, and an Eastwood teacher returned to her home in Wimbledon – but historic events on 8 and 9 May were suitably inscribed in red ink and capital letters in the logbooks: 'VICTORY IN EUROPE. SCHOOL CLOSED FOR TWO DAYS' NATIONAL HOLIDAY.' Somebody at Holycroft Junior School added a note of the length of the war – '5 yrs. 9 mths.' – but didn't get it quite right!

Hitler, who was easy to caricature, was popularly burnt in effigy. Street parties were held, despite indifferent weather. Rawling Street children sat down to potted-meat sandwiches, jelly and a victory cake; and at Back Rupert Street the oldest resident dressed up as John Bull and 'marched the children round the neighbourhood'. People danced at night in the Town Hall Square. In the midst of the festivities, at the High Street roundabout, a lorry laden with victory beer shed four barrels (which burst) and a lot of bottles (which broke). 'A large quantity of beer covered the roadway', mourned a rueful observer, 'and escaped down the drains'.

On a more serious note, a battalion of the Durham Light Infantry, then stationed in Keighley, paraded for a thanksgiving service in Victoria Park, and a wreath in memory of their lost 50 officers and 500 men was laid on the War Memorial.

On the whole, the special services and concerts came slightly later, on Sunday 13 May, or when the schools had got back into their stride again. At Eastwood Junior School the scholars took part in a Victory Pageant, and at Holycroft they collected £2 13s for the Soldiers', Sailors' and Airmen's Families Association. All the churches and chapels held services of thanksgiving; an especially large one in the Municipal Hall was accompanied

VE-Day: a battalion of the Durham Light Infantry lays a wreath on the War Memorial. Buglers from the Keighley Sea Cadets sounded Last Post and Reveille. *(Keighley Reference Library)*

by the Keighley Police Male Voice Prize Choir. This service included a detail that it was well to remember, at a time of general rejoicing, in the shape of 'a special prayer for our boys in the East and for those who have given loved ones for our freedom'.

At last the *Keighley News* felt able to give wartime details until then forbidden for security reasons (it had not even been able to report that the town had *not* been bombed!). Total Borough war savings of nearly £10,000,000 were unlikely to have surprised readers who had been keeping count, but the sum of £16,000-worth of salvage may have done. For the first time in print the tanks of the Royal Armoured Corps were described as 'racing up and down the streets of Keighley

almost as freely as public service vehicles' ('even yet the condition of some of the roads and the kerb edges stands as evidence of their presence').

For the first time too, the public was told how 'tons and tons of food for Britain's larder came to Keighley for storage purposes and most of the empty mills in the district were requisitioned for this purpose. The Army has also had a big medical store here.'

The odd bomb, probably jettisoned, had fallen in September 1940 near Cross Roads and Harbour Lodge on Haworth Moor, but 'the closest experience to actual blitz', ran the tale which had lost none of its drama in the five years of its telling, 'came in August, 1940, when the Luftwaffe visited Bradford, and hundreds of Keighley people will never forget the sound of the falling bombs or the fearsome glares in the skies from the burning buildings in Bradford.'

Photographer George A. Shore obviously told everybody to smile, but these workers had good reason to be happy – it was the summer of 1945 and the Second World War had just ended. They worked in the inspection department at the Royal Ordnance Factory at Steeton, where Mr Shore was taking advantage of a relaxation of photographic restrictions (outdoors at least). The lady fourth from the left at the front appears to have been squashed in at the last moment, and a girl at the top left is leaning forward because she thinks she may be off the edge of the picture. *(George A. Shore/Mrs J. McNamara)*

The fortunes of war, it turned out, had thrown up some bizarre episodes. When Flying Officer Kenneth Stanley Butterfield had flown a Walrus Amphibian to within sight of the French coast to rescue a downed Spitfire pilot

Photographer William Speight was also posing Royal Ordnance Factory groups around the end of the war. These administrative staff (well over a hundred) represent only a fraction of the 4,000 and more employed at 'The Dump'. *(William Speight/Mr Michael Shearing)*

Keighley Civil Defence members immaculately uniformed and posed in a wet-looking park. *(Keighley Reference Library)*

in 1943, his course was plotted in the operations room by the WAAF girl whom he had married at Riddlesden Church shortly before.

The Royal Ordnance Factory announced its forthcoming closure; it was to be used in future for the sorting and storage of wool. Some 200 evacuees went

Their Oxenhope Civil Defence colleagues look rather more relaxed, however. This group constitutes a veritable 'Who Was Who' in wartime Oxenhope, including such well-known names as Sydney Bancroft, Gawthorpe Holmes, Henry Raistrick, Tom Mason, John Heaton and Edna Murgatroyd. *(Mrs Clara S. Feather)*

Victory parties after the surrender of Japan were spread over several weeks. Here the women and children (and one old man) of Bradford Road and Back Florist Street celebrate with tea and decorations on 25 August 1945. They had scrubbed the street before setting up the

tables. George A. Shore went round photographing all the parties. *(George A. Shore/Mrs Frank Mitchell)*

home, though another 150 from London and 40 from Hull, who had no homes to go to, had to remain in billets.

The Guernsey contingent left for home amid touching farewell scenes at Cross Roads. Schoolmaster Walter Brehaut wrote a letter of warmest thanks, not least to the Deputy Chief Billeting Officer who had 'so ably piloted' his party to Southampton. 'Our one regret voiced by all the evacuees as the ship left the dock leaving our friend a lonely figure waving us farewell on the quayside', he wrote, 'was that he could not accompany us on the last stage of the journey'.

At the General Election that July Keighley followed the national trend. The combined votes for Liberal Norman Robson, a local journalist in London, and glamorous Wing Commander H.A. Dalrymple-White, DFC and Bar, 'the National Conservative and Active Service Candidate', failed to match the 22,222 votes that swept Ivor Thomas back into Parliament (he was to resign from the Labour Party in 1947 and move through Independent status to the Conservatives, but that is another story).

With victory achieved in Europe, there was an increasing tendency to wind down. On a June Sunday the Keighley Division of the Civil Defence Wardens' Service held their last parade, marching from Lund Park to the Municipal Hall, where County Controller S.J. McVicar assured them that 'had the enemy visited Keighley, he would have found the area well prepared for him'. They were also assured that they had all 'been of one large family'. Their final act was to sing the National Anthem.

In July Keighley Town Council, which had been holding daytime meetings for the duration, decided to revert to evenings, as before the war. By August the next crop of victory bonfires had already been built, but for many the Second World War was not yet over. The local branch of the British Legion tactfully paid for an announcement on the front page of the *Keighley News*: 'To those Men and Women still serving in H.M. Forces at Home and Abroad, we say – "Well Done and Thank You."'

The eventual end of the war with Japan was recorded, as succinctly as anywhere, in oddly enough the minute-book of Knowle Park Congregational Church: 'The first announcement of the surrender of Japan which was unconditional was made at midnight on Tuesday August 14 by the Prime Minister, Mr Attlee, who suggested that the two following days should be observed as national holidays.' Knowle Park celebrated with a thanksgiving service the following Sunday, at which they sang 'national hymns'.

When the news reached Keighley, that midnight of 14 August, Marks and Spencer's staff were just finishing their dance in the Municipal Hall. They promptly organised an hour's extension, then adjourned into the Town Hall Square accompanied by their band. Joined by passing revellers, they carried on dancing till three in the morning! Meanwhile groups were singing in the streets and the Parish Church bells rang a victory peal. At Oakworth that midnight Lane Ends residents danced outside to a gramophone, reinforced by a piano and a fiddle.

Wednesday 15 August was christened VJ1-Day. Surprisingly, some didn't know the war was finally over until they got to work. Up went the flags and bunting, Back Aireworth Street maintaining its tradition for outstanding decorations, but the Keighley climate soon put a damper on festivities. Haworth Public Prize Band played in the Town Hall Square 'until rained off', while an open-air dance in Haworth Park had to retreat into the Senior Council School. Not everybody got a holiday. The Keighley Industrial Co-operative Society Ltd held a board meeting on the Thursday – VJ2-Day – at which their manager grimly reported that 'the complete staff walked out at noon V.J. Day (1) from Ingrow Lane Branch'. On the other hand, some butchering, fish, grocery, dairy and clerical staff had remained at their posts all day, and were rewarded with 'time and a quarter rates' or a holiday in lieu.

In general, street parties started on VJ2-Day, but some were postponed owing to poor weather or to allow more time for preparations. At Back Aireworth Street ninety ate 'sandwiches, veal, potted meat, custards, jellies, blancmange, and cakes and buns'. Beechcliffe children were treated to 'a real pre-war tuck-in'. Centre-piece at Thorn Street, Parkwood, was a two-tier iced

The forecourt of Lund Park Methodist Church provided an ideal setting for these residents of the Malsis Road area when they held their Victory party on 18 August 1945. A noticeable feature of such groups is the absence of men. These children look to have thrived on their wartime rations. *(Mrs Elsie Dean)*

There are many carefully posed photographs of street Victory parties, but this less formal snapshot captures a child's-eye view from the end of a table in Tufton Street, Silsden, in September 1945. (*Mrs Edna Throup*)

cake in red, white and blue inscribed 'Peace and Victory in 1945'. Redcliffe Street burned 'an effigy of Tojo'.

There were many bonfires, some lit prematurely on the Tuesday midnight. At Oakworth on VJ2-Day they had a 'monster' one in Slaymaker Plantation. As 350 children had each been given a parcel of fireworks, this must have been a spectacular affair. Yate Lane, Oxenhope, featured what was described as the 'lusty' singing of *There'll Always Be an England*.

The street parties continued through August, and even into September. George A. Shore, a freelance photographer who also sold linoleum and carpet squares in Keighley Market, tried to record them all. At Coldshaw they had to have four sittings-down, attended by the Haworth Victory Queen. In Mill Hey Methodist schoolroom each child was given an apple, a bar of chocolate, ice-cream and 1s 2d.

Steeton, meanwhile, remained relatively unruffled by the mid-August events, for both Dixons' and Cloughs' mills were closed for the annual holiday. Wartime 'stay-at-home' holidays had been discontinued, and Steeton folk had seized the opportunity for their first real break for years. Some 200 villagers had gone to Blackpool for the week, and another 200 to Morecambe. Ten were at Bridlington, twelve at Liverpool, three at Scarborough and three at Southport. Steeton seemed comparatively deserted.

Thanksgiving services were universal on Sunday 19 August, the Mayor, Town Council and members of wartime organisations attending that at Keighley Parish Church. Between 13 and 20 October the Keighley Savings Committee hosted a Thanksgiving Week, which featured a feast of celebrations: a Grand Thanksgiving Ball, an Old-Time Victory Ball, a Modern Victory Ball, a Monster Children's Party, a Schools Festival, a Grand Victory Revue. . . . The underlying object, of course, was to raise National Savings funds. The week's total for Keighley was £651,512, of which £224,737 came from smaller savers.

Haworth held a Peace Celebration Week in September, opened by their Victory Queen and offering prizes for street decorations. Its official handbook revealed that almost 600 Haworth men and over 100 women had served in His Majesty's Forces, of whom 39 'gave their lives or were reported missing'. The village had played host to some 90 adult and 270 child evacuees.

A highlight of the Week was *The Victor's Crown: The Story of Our Motherland*, an ambitious historical pageant produced by Harold G. Mitchell, curator of the Brontë Museum. 'A little boy and girl are sat listening to a story being read to them by their mother,' the programme summarised, 'when there is a knock on the door. As the children open the door Father Time introduces himself, and thence onward the story of the Victor's Crown is gradually unfolded by the action of the play.' Characters included John Bull, Florence Nightingale, a soldier, sailor and airman, and Young and Old England, plus tableaux representing 'Our Colonial Empire'.

More prisoners of war came home. Able Seaman Anthony Donisthorpe had lived for three and a half years in a bamboo hut in the Dutch East Indies on a diet of rice, potato tops, cats and dogs. 'My wife has kept a pair of silk stockings I sent her from Capetown back in 1941,' said one returned inmate of the notorious Changi Gaol in Singapore. 'She is going to wear them for the first time today.'

There was a spate of 'Welcome Home' dinners. The British Legion dreamed of a Memorial Building, 'a place where ex-Servicemen with their wives and children and ex-Servicewomen may meet for social fellowship'. But these were brief respites from such postwar problems as the housing shortage. 'Tragic stories relating to overcrowding and insanitary housing conditions continue to reach the Department,' complained the Medical Officer of Health in 1945, 'with little prospect of anything being done to meet their amelioration'.

German prisoners of war were controversially employed on building the Bracken Bank Council Estate (some housewives gave them sandwiches, which

An aftermath of war: prefabricated homes on the Woodhouse Estate, photographed when still occupied in 1961. They were demolished two years later. *(Keighley News/Keighley Reference Library)*

disgusted some ex-servicemen). Delivery of prefabricated homes was delayed, and it was April 1946 before Keighley's first fifty Tarran Mark IV temporary houses went up at Bracken Bank, to be followed by another forty-five at Woodhouse.

Assuredly, victory did not mean an instant return to ease and plenty. As the darker nights approached, Keighley Town Council had to decree that, apart from road intersections and danger-spots, street lights would only be turned on half an hour after the standard lighting-up time and then be turned off at midnight. This – one more difficulty among many – was 'in view of the serious problem of maintaining supplies of fuel during next winter'.

Society itself had changed. Out of the turmoil of Eastern Europe came a sad new immigration known as European Volunteer Workers, or more brutally but accurately Displaced Persons. By 1947 there were nearly 600 of them at the Howden Hall Hostel alone. There the Ukrainians among them put on an exhibition of needlework and woodcarving, while an International Revue at the Municipal Hall featured singers from the National Opera of Kiev, a Polish raconteur, a Ukrainian dancer, a Hungarian pianist – and Mary Murphy from Ireland.

'I could write a book about them,' wrote a local civil servant, 'and the title of that book would be: "Tragedy!"' He compiled a scrapbook of some of their letters to his office. G. Pataky, lodging in Keighley and labouring in a textile mill, had been 'a professional officer, a parachutist captain in the former Hungarian Royal Army'; now he had 'a good mind to learn the weaving'. Wanda Sztejnke, who worked at John Haggas Ltd, knew only Polish and German but got somebody to write her poignant request:

My husband Jan Sztejnke was all the time in transit camp Market Harborough. Now because we want to be together, he has come to me, and Mr Haggas promised him employment in his firm the onliest difficulty being lodgings. We tried to get a room but in vein, because it is very difficult to get lodgings here in Keighley. So we have come to you and would be very thankful if you could help us and settle him down somewhere, for instance Silsden where, I heard, are some vacancies. If that is not possible, we both want to be sent back to a transit camp, Full Sutton for instance, because we want to live and work together.

'The war is over; peace has come; but there is much work to be done,' a *Keighley News* editorial had observed in August 1945. Wyndham Rowland, editor since 1906, had nursed his newspaper through two world wars. An 'editor in the old tradition', never having used a typewriter and preparing all his copy by hand, he was a respected local voice:

. . . but there is much work to be done to replenish our own denuded stocks and to supply the needs of the suffering populations of other lands, without whose recovery we ourselves cannot hope to prosper. To this work we must set ourselves individually and collectively, with the same unity of purpose and unselfish determination to do our bit as our people have shown in the war that has now been brought to such a successful conclusion.

How far this ideal would be fulfilled, only time was to tell.

Index